GEORGE G. HUNTER III

Abingdon Press • *Nashville*

CHRISTIAN, EVANGELICAL, AND . . . DEMOCRAT?

This book is printed on acid-free paper.

Library of Congress Cataloging-in-Publication Data

Hunter, George G.
    Christian, Evangelical, and—Democrat? / George G. Hunter III.
      p. cm.
    ISBN 0-687-49489-3 (binding: adhesive perfect : alk. paper)
    1. Evangelistic work—United States. 2. Christianity and politics—United States.
    I. Title.

    BV3793.H8455 2006
    261.70973—dc22

                                                                2005037942

06 07 08 09 10 11 12 13 14 15—10 9 8 7 6 5 4 3 2 1

MANUFACTURED IN THE UNITED STATES OF AMERICA

To "Charley,"
the state senator who,
in one telephone call,
provoked this book into existence.

CONTENTS

Contents

FOREWORD

L ike Dr. George "Chuck" Hunter, I have voted for both Democratic and Republican candidates through the years, and I have done so, as he has, in an attempt to be true to my faith. Like Dr. Hunter, I have experienced something close to loathing from some of my fellow Christians who sensed that I didn't stick with the straight Republican Party line that they felt was the only path for committed Christians. Like Dr. Hunter, I have become more and more concerned that the civil language of respectful dialogue is being replaced, first by the shrill language of bitter argument, and then by the threatening language of insult and mockery. I, too, have been heartbroken to find Christians sometimes at the forefront of this shift.

I have listened to many conversations among young Christian leaders from evangelical backgrounds debating whether they should simply abandon the label "evangelical" altogether, because the meaning it now carries is more political than spiritual, and because it communicates an ethos with which they are ashamed to be associated. On many occasions I have watched the evening news on television and felt, as have many of my peers, that the spokespeople who are commonly chosen to represent Christianity in general or evangelicalism in particular simply don't speak for me.

Meanwhile, I have heard these religious leaders repeatedly portray themselves as oppressed victims of a vast left-wing conspiracy, in spite of the dominance they enjoy in all branches of government.

Sometimes all of this has discouraged me (perhaps *depressed* is the more accurate word) as I have wondered why alternate voices don't speak up more often. I know these voices are out there, but only a few (Jim Wallis, Tony and Bart Campolo, and a small number of others) ever stand up to the dominant religious establishment. Eventually I started speaking up myself and quickly found out why the number of those who do likewise is so small: faith communities have subtle ways of silencing dialogue and enforcing monologue. Dr. Hunter now joins that small but growing group who are breaking the monologue's monopoly. He will suffer for it, I imagine, but I don't think he will be dissuaded.

He is an ideal person to take this courageous step. His credentials as an evangelical are impeccable. His rootedness in thoughtful Christian theology and constructive ministry engagement are beyond question. Not only that, but he is to the bone an educator; he writes and speaks with clarity and directness that can stimulate both GED's and Ph.D.'s. People who have only heard the monologue will feel, as they read these pages, that they are finally learning the other side of the story.

Several of Dr. Hunter's books have helped me a great deal through the years. *How to Reach Secular People* and *The Celtic Way of Evangelism* are two of my favorites. This volume, I predict, will become his most widely read book yet because of its courage, clarity, and timeliness.

For too long the polarization between the Religious Right and the secular left has paralyzed us. Our need is not simply for a Religious Left, although that might be part of the solution. What we need most now is Christians in both major parties, and other "third" parties too, who commit themselves to raise the level of discourse above bitter argument, mutual caricaturing, and divisive win-lose politics. We need committed Christians who care for the common good, who seek to be uniters rather than dividers, in deed and not just in word, who let their faith modify their politics rather than the reverse, who are suspicious of "graven ideologies," and who love their political counterparts by refusing to see them as enemies, treating them instead as beloved neighbors. We need people of faith who search the Scriptures, not for proof-texts to support the policies about which they've already made up their minds, but rather for new truths that will stretch their political and social understandings beyond the planks of any party.

That describes Dr. Hunter's aim in this important and well-written book.

In spite of the word "Democrat" in the title, Dr. Hunter isn't interested in getting Republicans to switch parties. He wants to help Christians—and especially evangelical Christians—see that their first loyalty is to a King and kingdom higher than any "principality or power" on earth. If we get that straight, we can expect a revolution of goodness and peace to continually unfold. The effects of that revolution will make themselves felt in the areas of economics, ecology, sexuality and family, poverty, education, the arts, racial reconciliation, the media, religion, and yes, even politics.

—Brian D. McLaren

INTRODUCTION

Is it possible, even remotely, that a serious Christian could be both an "evangelical" and a "Democrat"? Once, until fairly recently, the answer would have been an obvious "yes"; Billy Graham was (and is) a prominent example. Today, however, putting "evangelical" and "Democrat" in the same sentence sounds, to most Americans, like an "oxymoron"—a figure of speech in which we yoke two terms (now) assumed to be contradictory.

Many people find oxymorons stimulating; some people even collect them. The websites devoted to oxymorons feature expressions like "jumbo shrimp," "civil engineer," "business ethics," "Microsoft Works," "instant classic," and "cold as hell." The names of some sports teams are oxymoronic—like the University of Pennsylvania Quakers are sometimes referred to as the "Fighting Quakers"; and there are the Wake Forest "Demon Deacons." (Some Baptist pastors report, however, that "demon" and "deacon" are not at all contradictory.) Oxymorons often surface in conversation about religion; people have referred to "Christian Scientists," "devout atheists," and "United Methodists."

The war in Iraq has occasioned oxymorons old and new, such as "military intelligence," "war games," "just war," "peace force," "volunteer army," and "friendly fire." Some Democrats suspect that "compassionate conservatism" and "Black Republicans" are oxymoronic, as well as Mr. Bush's "working vacations"! Thoughtful people in both parties have recently grouped "intelligent talk radio" with the more established oxymorons. I am proposing that the time has come to reintroduce "Christian evangelical Democrats" into our lexicons.

"Everyone knows" today that, in political matters, evangelical Christianity has become "the Republican Party at prayer." The prevailing paradigm connects conservative politics and conservative religion closer than Siamese twins. But *is* the evangelical-Republican connection a compelling one for all Christians who emphasize second birth, and evangelism and mission, for whom Scripture is the supreme authority? Do Republican policies, on every issue, necessarily follow from a careful, obedient reading of the Biblical Revelation?

Indeed, *could* one be an "evangelical Democrat"? Increasingly, evangelical Christians who think "outside of the box" are employing words not usually associated with each other. The undisputed champion in this trend is Brian McLaren; the subtitle of his book promises to explain "Why I Am a missional + evangelical + post/protestant + liberal/conservative + mystical/poetic + biblical + charismatic/contemplative + fundamentalist/ calvinist + anabaptist/anglican + methodist + catholic + green + incarnational + depressed-yet-hopeful + emergent + unfinished Christian"![1]

In case a reader wants to know my background or my "agenda," I have voted in nine presidential elections—five times for the Democrat and four times for the Republican. That record would qualify me (if for anything) as a bipartisan "Republocrat." In recent years, however, I have supported Democrats more often than Republicans, partly because I believe in some things that Republicans used to believe in, but have since abdicated (or no longer prioritize)—such as conservation, civil rights, infrastructure,[2] gun control, balanced budgets, states' rights, and a serious presumption against initiating warfare—that Democrats now believe in more than Republicans. (I will unpack several of those themes later.) My "agenda" is to encourage evangelical Christians to (once again) love Democrats as well as Republicans, and to be involved as "salt" and "light" in both parties (once again), and to invite pre-Christian Democrats (and Republicans) to become followers of Christ. I want to change the prevailing paradigm, essentially by helping us rediscover an earlier one.[3]

NOTES

1. Brian D. McLaren, *A Generous Orthodoxy: Why I Am a missional + evangelical + post/protestant + liberal/conservative + mystical/poetic + biblical + charismatic/contemplative + fundamentalist/calvinist + anabaptist/anglican + methodist + catholic + green + incarnational + depressed-yet-hopeful + emergent + unfinished Christian* (Grand Rapids, Mich.: Zondervan, 2004).

2. The outstanding historical example of "planned infrastructure" is Eisenhower's development of the USA's interstate highway system. The term generally refers to the nation's road, railway, airline, and other transportation systems, as well as water, electricity, mail, telephone, telegraph, Internet, and other systems upon which most of the nation's people depend.

3. I am not the only writer trying to call evangelical Christians to reclaim Christianity's full ethical vision. Leaders like Ron Sider, Tony Campolo, and Jim Wallis were engaging this challenge long before it occurred to me to wade in. Wallis's *God's Politics* was published when this project neared completion, so I have not depended on that new source.

HOW MOST AMERICAN EVANGELICALS BECAME ONE-PARTY PEOPLE

In the 1950s through the 1970s, I knew many evangelical Christian leaders who were card-carrying Democrats and many who were Republicans. Evangelical Christian leaders were involved—and influential—with both major parties (local, state, and national); they conversed, loved, and prayed with people of both parties, and they worked (often with success) to influence both parties toward policies closer to our understanding of God's purposes. Billy Graham visibly modeled an evangelical policy and strategy of bipartisan influence.

The 1980 presidential election suddenly revealed that this *de facto* strategy (which actually predated Mr. Graham for more than a century) had shifted to the Right, big time. Most evangelical Christian leaders abandoned Jimmy Carter (well-known to be a "born-again Christian") and supported Ronald Reagan (a generic Protestant who did not profess second birth). While Carter's four-year term had produced some reasons to consider another candidate (like high inflation and the United States' boycott of the Moscow Olympics), and Reagan had been a good-enough

California governor to consider on merit, we now know that Reagan's election signaled a sudden and major evangelical shift from two-party influence to one-party support. The surveys fluctuate slightly, but today more than 75 percent of professing "evangelical Christians" now classify themselves as Republicans.

In the last generation, American society's most visible television evangelicals—such as Jerry Falwell, who launched The Moral Majority (1979), and Pat Robertson, who established the Christian Coalition (1989)—have identified with the Republican Party exclusively. The lines redrawn in the 1980s have endured, and fueled by public evangelicals like Falwell, Robertson, James Kennedy, and James Dobson, several megachurch pastors, columnists like Cal Thomas, and radio pundits like Rush Limbaugh, the lines have hardened. Furthermore, the gap has widened, to the point that most evangelicals (and most Americans) now assume that in political, economic, and social matters, evangelical Christianity can have simply (and only) a conservative Republican perspective, in which even "moderate" Republicans are suspect.

The intensity has escalated, as well as rage, hatred, and character assassination. The public evangelicals (and the Republican Party, at least during campaigns), it seems, no longer consider ideas they do not agree with as worth public discussion; they do what they can to derogate or destroy the sources of "heretical" ideas. And no one on the Right (or on the Left), it seems, ever accurately summarizes or characterizes the other group's point of view. So, propagandists on the Right now label "pro-choice" people as "pro-abortion," and environmentalists as "tree huggers," and people who are reluctant to privatize Social Security as "Bush bashers." (Partisans on the Left, of course, are not incapable of distortion propaganda.)

Evangelical Christians who still support any causes that Democrats support now know that they are vulnerable; someone on the Right may, at any moment, unilaterally dismiss them from the kingdom of God, and publicly demonize them. The evangelical Right has not yet explicitly branded the Democratic Party as the party of the antichrist, but the mood and the moves are in that direction. Many evangelical churches now excommunicate people who voted Democrat, usually by ostracizing them, but occasionally by explicit church policy.

I am writing this book now—at whatever personal risk— because I believe the situation in the United States is now at a critical, perhaps perilous, time. All of the issues we are struggling with are more complex than any of the sloganeering (from the Right or the Left) can do justice to. All of the people who are politically involved (in either party) matter to God, and all of the people who are affected by public policy matter to God; therefore, all people who are politically involved or affected ought to matter to all branches of Christ's church.

I am concerned for the future of the two-party system, as well as for the (constitutionally mandated) healthy checks and balances in government and also for the freedom of the press. For the first time in our nation's history, there is a serious, persistent, lavishly funded campaign to achieve, and then institutionalize, one-party rule over the executive, legislative, and judicial branches—in the federal government and in most of the states— and to intimidate the press into silence or actual subservience to the ruling party. We do not need to ask how that crusade would turn out. Lord Acton's reflection that "Power tends to corrupt and absolute power corrupts absolutely" is no mere theory. Give one-party rule a little time, and corruption, nepotism, and incompetence will charge into any community, state, or nation in which one party gains monopoly. If you doubt this claim, visit any nation (or state or almost any city) with only one powerful party and a party-controlled media, then ask yourself if you'd recommend that arrangement for any other nation, including the United States.

Republican control of the White House for most of the last four decades has facilitated the greatest transfer of wealth in the country's history. In 1980, CEOs were paid, on average, 42 times the salary of the average worker; today, they are paid 476 times the salary of the average worker. Yet public evangelicals perceive no problem worth mentioning. As I write this, the public evangelicals argue that seven Republican appointees out of nine

Supreme Court justices and Republican-appointee majorities on ten of the thirteen federal appeals courts are not enough. They now campaign for monopoly control of the judiciary.

I am especially concerned for the soul and the credibility of evangelical Christianity in this land. Many of our most public "evangelical" spokespersons do not fully represent Christianity, and Christianity's vision for the world, to the pre-Christian populations of the United States. Many educated pagans, for instance, have figured out that some of the public spokespersons of evangelical Christianity have "sold out" on Jesus' Sermon on the Mount. I submit that evangelical Christianity is an apostolic movement entrusted both with the Lord's mandate to be "fishers" of men and women and to make disciples among all peoples AND the imperative to work for a just world for people (and God's other creatures) to live in. Two indispensable objectives in our public role, therefore, are to build all the bridges possible to lost people who need to be found and to accurately and fully represent the Christian faith and ethic when we represent it.

CHAPTER TWO

WHAT AMERICAN EVANGELICALS CAN LEARN FROM WORLD EVANGELICALS

Like "Mary of old," I have pondered these matters in my heart for some time. I am now proposing some reflections for understanding evangelical Christianity's present and future mission in this land. Let's begin with one premise: there is no necessary connection between conservative (or orthodox, or evangelical) Christian theology and conservative policies on all political, economic, social, and international matters—nor, for that matter, between liberal theology and liberal policies.

We need look no further than Christianity in other nations to find scores of examples. In the European history of the last three centuries, for instance, most of the state churches (such as the Church of England) have been theologically left of center and politically right of center on most issues; most of Europe's "free" or "nonconformist" churches (such as the Baptist or Methodist churches) have been theologically right of center while advocating policies to the left of center on most issues. So, in eighteenth-century England, several free churches and a wing of the Anglican Church led by William Wilberforce battled the slave trade until the House of Commons outlawed it across the British Empire. John Wesley and his Methodists supported Wilberforce, while championing many progressive social reforms for England's urban poor. In early twentieth-century England, evangelist and pastor Hugh Price Hughes became involved with the urban issues that Dickens's novels dramatized; Hughes's movement, the "Nonconformist Conscience," reminded his country that "what is morally wrong cannot be politically right."

Generally, the pattern we observe in England is consistent with the pattern of evangelical Christianity in many nations. Evangelical Christian leaders are usually "progressive" and active on most of the issues that matter to the people's general welfare. I know of only five types of exceptions, globally, to this generalization: (1) churches that expect Christ to return soon and to consummate his promised kingdom supernaturally have no drive to work politically for a better future; (2) churches whose belief in divine sovereignty leads them to conclude that humans are powerless to work for a society's improvement refrain from political involvement; (3) churches living in total-itarian societies often find attempts at political influence diffi-cult, or impossible, or even suicidal; (4) churches in societies where Christians are a negligible minority usually know that, for now, they have little (or no) political influence because they lack the "critical mass" of people needed to exercise influence; and (5) the United States of America and only since about 1980. For most of our history, American Christianity has been like it usually is elsewhere—progressive on most of the issues that really mattered within the Christian ethic. The nineteenth-century evangelist Charles G. Finney led the Second Great Awakening *and* was a national leader in the cause to abolish slavery. Some of Finney's contemporaries (and detractors) thought that becoming a Christian was, for Finney, becoming a follower of Jesus Christ *and* becoming an abolitionist. (He *did* sometimes invite converts to sign antislavery pledge cards.) A half-century later, William Jennings Bryan (the era's best known public evangelical) championed a range of politically progressive causes that were rooted in evangelical Christian conviction. As Woodrow Wilson's secretary of state, for instance, Bryan opposed war because he believed that Jesus opposed war. Beginning in the 1950s (*before* the Supreme Court mandated school desegregation in *Brown vs. the Board of Education of Topeka, Kansas*), Billy Graham integrated his crusades and catalyzed reconciliation between America's races.

By about 1980, however, a generation of American evangelical leaders had lost much of the ethical vision that had usually driven their predecessors for most of our history, and still drives most evangelicals in the other lands where reform is possible. In this same period, many evangelical laypeople, whose ancestors had been progressive Christian Democrats, moved up the social ladder, became estranged from (or embarrassed by) their social roots, and became Republicans. For the last generation, American public evangelicalism has behaved much more like the European state churches—siding with the social, political, and corporate "Establishment," working to enforce good citizenship as establishment people define it.

Underneath the (well-funded) public face, of course, American evangelical Christians are more broadly committed than they are portrayed in the media. Calvin College, for instance, is one of the strongest evangelical Christian colleges in the country. In a poll of their faculty in 2001, 25 percent of Calvin College's faculty reported themselves as politically liberal, 45 percent as centrist, and 28 percent as conservative. As this is written, *The Washington Times* (May 17, 2005) reports that President George W. Bush agreed to speak for Calvin's 2005 spring commencement. Many professors surfaced to declare that Christians are called to restore creation and pursue justice and to be "peacemakers" who initiate war "only as a *last* resort." One history professor declared, "We are not Lynchburg . . . Our faith trumps political ideology." (In the future, I submit, *many* more evangelicals will be thinking for themselves in public matters.)

⊷ ⊷ ⊷

How, and why, did much of American evangelical Christianity depart from the ethical vision of our predecessors *and* become the "odd man out" in world Christianity? How did our public evangelicalism get to this point? More important, how can we make sense of where evangelical Christianity in America is today and identify some steps toward greater public faithfulness and effectiveness? The next four chapters will demonstrate that much of our current situation and future hope is better understood from four perspectives: (a) Christianity's gospel and ethic, (b) the history of Christianity's stewardship of its gospel and ethic, (c) an understanding of where many of the ideas that drive us *really* come from, and (d) an understanding of how we communicate (or mis-communicate) our beliefs and convictions publicly.

CHAPTER THREE

CHRISTIANITY'S GOSPEL AND ITS ETHIC

C hristianity came into the ancient world communicating a "gospel"[1] for all people; all people had the inalienable right to understand and respond to this good news. What became the Christian movement was launched when Jesus of Nazareth engaged the people of first-century Galilee with the good news that the long-promised kingdom (or active reign) of God was now beginning to break into human history. "The time is fulfilled, and the kingdom of God has come near, repent, and believe in the good news" (Mark 1:15). Some of the people, through their openness to God, especially perceived God's action as Jesus forgave sins, cast out demons, and healed a range of diseases, and proclaimed the gospel "as one having authority," and not as the Jewish scribes.[2] In (what the Christian tradition calls) "the Lord's Prayer," Jesus taught that our cooperation with God's kingdom especially involved obeying the will of God—not merely in the old sense of obeying God's laws or instructions, but in a new sense of following God's Spirit as he leads and empowers us for fulfilling his purposes.

Jesus employed many parables to help people discover a fuller meaning of God's kingdom, and as he befriended sinners and many types of people on the margins of Jewish society and as he engaged in many ministries and in actions such as the cleansing of the Temple, he was also dramatizing the kingdom's meaning. He emphasized that God's reign had only begun to break into human history, in the sense that a new day at 7:00 a.m. has only dawned; God's promised kingdom will be consummated later, when Christ will return and the will of God will "be done, on earth as it is in heaven." In the meantime, we live in the history between the kingdom's launch and its full completion. Foreknowledge of the time when God's kingdom will be completed, however, has not been entrusted to us (Acts 1:6-7).

Jesus' message aroused the antagonism of the Jews and Romans; they were invested in the status quo and were not open to an "upside down kingdom" in which the last would be first and people of good will would inherit the earth. So they conspired against the source of this disturbing message, and they executed him by crucifixion, and his followers scattered and were vanquished. When, however, God raised Jesus from death, and Jesus commissioned his disciples to scatter to all peoples with the gospel and then sent the Holy Spirit to unite and empower them, the gospel's meaning expanded enormously.

From the gospel *of* Jesus that focused essentially on the kingdom of God, his movement's gospel *about* Jesus Christ now took on many themes. The church now explicitly proclaimed what had been more implicit in Jesus' teaching and ministry—that Jesus was (and is) Israel's promised Messiah.[3] "Jesus is Lord" emerged as the movement's first creedal affirmation. The symbol of the fish caught on early and widely,[4] as well as the symbol of the cross. His followers believed he was the supreme revelation of God *and* of what humans were meant to be. No one theme could now communicate the larger gospel's full meaning, so the gospel became like a mosaic of truth claims, or a gem with many different facets. It became, for instance, good news about the grace[5] of God, and the righteousness[6] of God, and the love[7] of God, and the peace[8] of God and the restoration of the image of God in people who turned to God. It became a gospel of the forgiveness of sins and new birth,[9] reconciliation[10] and redemption,[11] justification[12] and salvation[13] and sanctification,[14] abundant life and eternal life,[15] a new covenant and a new community and a new humanity, a new heaven and a new earth.

The gospel gem includes, as one prominent facet, the good news that Christ's death and resurrection have defeated the power of death (humanity's final enemy) and that Christ has preceded us in heaven to prepare a place for us. However, in contrast to the ancient mystery religions and Gnostic religions (as should be clear from the multiple themes in the last paragraph), Christianity is not only about going to heaven—though, today, many people assume it is only about that, or almost so. (Nineteenth-century Holiness evangelists used to remind their people that even this part of the gospel was not about "gitting" us to heaven, but about "fitting" us for heaven.) Finally, Jesus' own leading edge of the gospel that emphasized the kingdom of God has remained a large, bright, and central piece of the gospel mosaic through much of Christian history.

The gospel we know in Scripture is, however, much more than a sum total of themes. The gospel is rooted in historical *events*, most notably the liberation of the Hebrew people from their slavery in Egypt and the resurrection of Jesus of Nazareth from death. Without the Exodus, there would be no Judaism; without the Exodus and the Resurrection, there would be no Christianity. The gospel is also rooted in the *experiences* of the people of God. Following their exodus from Egypt, the Hebrew people experienced the God of Abraham with them, as a cloud by day and a pillar of fire by night; the disciples lived with Jesus and observed his ministries and miracles, and following his resurrection, their hearts burned within them as he walked with them and opened to them the Scriptures. The gospel is also *narrative*. All four Gospel writers report many of the stories that Jesus told, and they tell the story of what God was up to in the Christ Event; that story is the center in the grand narrative that begins with creation and tells the long story of Israel and the early history of the New Israel, and ends with the promise that God's kingdom will be consummated. Finally, the gospel is also a *perspective*. Christianity's truth claims are given not merely that we might believe them, but that we can perceive life and the world through

11

the lenses of New Testament faith. (C. S. Lewis once suggested that we don't need more books about Christianity as much as we need more books about other things from a Christian perspective.)

———⚬⚬⚬——— ———⚬⚬⚬——— ———⚬⚬⚬———

Jesus' interpretation of God's kingdom built strongly on the shoulders of God's earlier revelations through the Hebrew prophets, who (contrary to much current evangelical lore) were not primarily predictors of the future but revealers of the will of God; they represented Israel's God demanding that his people turn from their idolatry and that they cooperate with God's vision for justice and peace. Amos (5:21-24 NIV) declared, for instance, that unless God's people "let justice roll on like a river," their empty worship services and praise songs would offend their God. Micah 6:8 tells us that God essentially wants people of faith "to do justice, and to love kindness, and to walk humbly with your God." Several of the prophets especially exposed, as one type of idolatry, the Hebrew people's periodic inclination to puff up with nationalistic pride. Jesus stood, unmistakably, in the tradition of the Hebrew prophets.

Jesus, however, extended God's revelation beyond what the prophets comprehended. Prophets like Isaiah sometimes understood that God has raised up Israel primarily to be a light to the Gentiles; Jonah (reluctantly) understood that Yahweh's compassion even extended to peoples quite unlike the Hebrew people—such as the barbarian Ninevites. Regarding Jesus' wider social vision, the church has usually known that the Sermon on the Mount (summarized in Matthew 5–7) is the greatest single treasury of the kingdom's ethical vision. So, for instance, the Lord's kingdom is especially for the poor, and people who are righteous, merciful, nonviolent, and peacemaking have prominent roles in the kingdom's work. Kingdom people are free from anxiety, and they no longer rely on wealth, anger, and revenge as approaches in life and human relations; indeed, they practice Jesus' Golden Rule in their human relations. The kingdom of God calls us to marital faithfulness, truth telling, love for enemies, and prayer in the pattern that Jesus taught to his first disciples. According to Jesus, kingdom people will know that creation's animals (and even the plants) matter to God, though people matter more. The way of the kingdom is a narrow way that mandates us to serve one Master only and to seek first the reign of God and God's righteousness in our lives and in the world. People who live in cooperation with God's presence and purpose are like the man who built his house upon solid rock; compared to life in the kingdom, all other lifestyles are as sinking sand.

— ∞ —   — ∞ —   — ∞ —

How does this comprehensive understanding of "the faith which was once delivered unto the saints" (Jude 3 KJV) help us reflect upon public evangelical Christianity in the United States today?

For one thing, it helps us see that the public face of evangelicalism represents less than a sufficiently full understanding of the Christian faith. Many of the public evangelicals feature only two or three facets of the gospel gem. To discover this fact for yourself, conduct a simple experiment. Listen to many of them for (say) twenty hours of radio or television, asking "What, according to them, is Christianity basically about? What does it stand for? What does it offer?" You will discover that the gospel, according to many public evangelicals, is only about going to heaven after we die, with forgiveness (for "sins of the flesh"), and new birth, and a life of many blessings thrown in to (allegedly) complete the picture. Many of the public evangelicals never even get around to sharing most of the gospel's themes that all people have an inalienable right to understand.

When some of the public evangelicals do attempt a more serious theological interpretation, they often convey only part of that piece of the gospel. So, for instance, they may be clearer about the "divinity" of Christ than they are about the true "humanity" of Christ. Again, I can seldom be sure that they are presenting the full triune doctrine of God to the American people; in what approaches a "Unitarianism" of the Second Person, or the Third Person, they feature Christ, or the Holy Spirit, much more than the other two persons of Christianity's triune God. Again, the atonement that was achieved for us by Christ's death on a cross is explained only as a substitution; Jesus died in our place, he paid the price for us, he "took the rap" for us. That is, indeed, wonderful news and part of the truth, but it ignores the Christian tradition's additional explanations—that Jesus also died in fulfillment of the Hebrew sacrificial tradition, that Jesus' death defeated the powers of evil and that his death was an extravagant demonstration of the love of God for sinners (Rom. 5:8).

While some of the public evangelicals "prophesy" about the future and the end of the age, they generally ignore the prophetic tradition about the will of God, and they almost never proclaim and interpret Jesus' own gospel of the kingdom of God that is now at hand, and they ignore the Sermon on the Mount's kingdom ethic *in toto.*

Take, as one example, the predisposition of many evangelical Christians to join uncritically in the slide from healthy patriotism, through unhealthy nationalism, into pathological idolatry. Nationalistic idolatry is, like gluttony, far too much of a good thing. Humanly speaking, patriotism is an understandable extension of the pride that most of us feel in our family, clan, community, people. A healthy patriotism provides the glue to hold a nation together. Its shared story and values bind its people together. People who do not love their country are not even motivated to pay their taxes. (By that criterion, many of the corporate leaders who pushed for "tax relief," and lobbied for tax loopholes, and insisted on tax credits when they moved several million jobs to other countries, may not really be patriotic!)

I love my country, and my periods of travel in other countries expose me to people who love their country also, and when I come home I have more reasons to love my country. "Patriotic Christianity," however, sometimes makes "Christian" the adjective and "patriotism" the noun, and a line has then been crossed into illusion, if not idolatry. John Smith, the Australian evangelist, was preaching in an evangelical church in the Philadelphia area. He had just visited the Liberty Bell and had read an inscription celebrating Philadelphia as the birthplace of freedom. While he expressed profound appreciation for the American Revolution, he reminded the people that it was Calvary, not Philadelphia, that witnessed the real birth of freedom. The people disagreed.

I am not a card-carrying academic historian, but I know that Christianity has been around a lot longer than my nation. (Actually, since the modern nation-state was basically an invention of the eighteenth-century European Enlightenment, Christianity has been around a lot longer than *any* nation.) From this perspective, and from the gospel's perspective, I experience discomfort when I hear politicians and evangelists wax on about the United States being the "greatest," and "We're number one!" My first impulse is to agree, but then I remember that I am hardly objective (I was, after all, socialized as an American) and that conclusions like "greatest" depend upon the criteria we use. So, when I hear reports that say things like the United States ranks forty-ninth among the world's nations in literacy, and thirty-seventh in health care, and forty-first in infant mortality, I wish we were spending more energy working for greatness and less energy claiming it.

The most serious indictment of extreme Christian patriotism is easily inferred from the song that many of us sang as Sunday school children, while we played in sandboxes:

> Jesus loves the little children,
> All the children of the world;
> Red and yellow, black and white,
> All are precious in his sight;
> Jesus loves the little children of the world.

If you still teach the children in your church to sing that song, you see the problem. (If your church no longer teaches that song to the children, your church might be the problem.) There is no nice way to say this: patriotism becomes idolatrous when it denies or ignores the real and full humanity of people who are citizens of other nation-states. Our government, our press, and our churches are all complicit in this sin. We share in it, for instance, every time we fixate on the number of Americans who died yesterday in Iraq or Afghanistan without reflecting on the number of Iraqis or Afghans who died. From what line of Christian reasoning do we assume that "our" people matter more than "their" people? How did we slide into any assumption other than the clear biblical teaching that *all* people are our brothers and sisters? Our doctrine of humanity genuinely matters. Our soldiers would be incapable of torturing a prisoner of war if they believed that the prisoner is our brother, who matters to God as we do. Arguably, some public evangelicals are the greatest propagandists for a sub-Christian doctrine of humanity. How could some of our most recognized public evangelicals have flunked "sandbox theology"?

Take, as another obvious example, the Christian's attitude toward war. Jesus told Pilate (John 18) that he would not allow his disciples to fight, even to protect him from arrest, trial, and execution, because "My kingdom is not from this world." The four Gospels in every place portray Jesus in the "pacifist" camp. In time, the historic church, while profoundly respecting what Jesus taught and modeled, experienced the need to formulate a faithful "Plan B." War may be occasionally necessary, as a last resort, but then only after prayerfully reflecting within the criteria for "just war."

While the military intervention in Afghanistan can be persuasively defended as a just war, the war in Iraq was launched in 2003 as a first resort, with no prior reflection within *either* the pacifist commitment *or* the careful just war line of moral reasoning and no clear understanding of what we were getting into. Soon after September 11, 2001, President Bush announced in a speech that our response to radical Muslims would be a "crusade." (Someone, presumably, informed him that, for reasons steeped in the long history between Christians and Muslims, that was the *worst* word to use, but, of course, Muslim radio stations and websites have been quoting from the speech ever since.) Some of the public evangelicals, however, have not departed from the war's first definition. They apparently assume that the wars in Afghanistan and in Iraq are both "crusades," validated by some "holy war" assumption that cannot be defended by any thoughtful tradition in the entire history of Christianity. Although they do not use the term, the intensity with which they defend the decision to go to war in Iraq and their quickness to brand Christian pacifist advocates and just war advocates as "unpatriotic" reveal a "holy war" agenda.

Almost every high school graduate, no matter how secular, knows that Jesus taught us to "love your enemies." The world, understandably, expects professing Christians to take that seriously, and the most theologically unsophisticated people would know that (among other things) Jesus probably meant for us to *not* humiliate, abuse, torture, and risk inflicting death upon prisoners of war—as some of our people have in Abu Ghraib prison and elsewhere.

Our government's spin and cover-up have, to date, placed virtually all the blame on soldiers at the lowest level. There is no reason to believe, however, that Lynndie England and her partners knew the insurgent soldiers' Arabic culture well enough to know what, of all possibilities, the prisoners would find most humiliating and degrading; their practices reflect directives from more informed people up the chain of command. We have no reason to exonerate people at the top. The White House announced, as policy, that the guidelines in the Geneva Conventions for the humane treatment of prisoners do not apply to the war against terrorists. The president announced that we should do "whatever it takes" to win the war against terrorism. (I recall it was reported widely that Mr. Bush explained to Senator Joe Biden in 2003, when the senator advised the president to consider the nuances of his decision, "I don't do nuance." That leaves the interpretation of "whatever it takes" up to the people implementing the directive.) "Whatever it takes" is, of course, not far from "The end justifies the means." (There is a distinction, but not a difference.) There was a time when we Christians understood that the idea of the ends justifying the means was the cardinal principle of ideological Communism's ethic, and we knew it was intrinsically and pervasively wrong.

In the summer of 2005, Senator Dick Durbin (Democrat from Illinois) suggested, in support of a proposed investigation, that the abuse of prisoners by American soldiers at Abu Ghraib and Guantanamo Bay was tragically reminiscent of the abuse of prisoners by the Third Reich, Stalin's Gulag, and the Pol Pot regime. Someone then engineered an orchestrated strategy to make Durbin the issue rather than prisoner abuse. The White House, the Pentagon, and others—including the Christian Coalition of America—called for the Democrats to support U.S. troops and demanded that the senator apologize to the American military and their families. Durbin caved in to the people who never apologize for anything, nor admit any mistakes, and apologized and declared our troops are "the greatest."

Whether or not Durbin *should* have apologized, the event has provided an opportunity to shed some light amidst the heat. Think about it. Our troops (or their ancestors) have come to the United States from many other nations—the United States is, after all, one of the most multiethnic nation-states on earth. That fact *might* suggest that the people who serve in our armed forces are more or less like people elsewhere and therefore susceptible to the same possibilities—for good or for evil.[16] Furthermore, my understanding of Christian theology would suggest that our armed forces (like any vocational population, such as politicians) would number some *bone fide* sinners in their ranks who, with opportunity and pressure, might engage in sin, including sin against a prisoner.

Senator Durbin's detractors, including the Christian Coalition, seemed to be acting in concert upon a remarkable assumption: that training and induction into the armed forces of the United States instill, in every soldier, sailor, and marine, a virtue and greatness that make their behavior morally exemplary and immune from appraisal. (In my mission travel, I have met too many "war babies," fathered by American military personnel, to find the assumption believable.) Think about it. They essentially claim that what centuries of Christian evangelism has achieved for only some people, schools like West Point and training centers like Quantico can achieve for everyone. Is it past time to quit denying the abuse of prisoners and support the movement to end it? Could it be time to apologize and repent? Could it even be time for the Christian Coalition, and other evangelicals, to recover the Christian doctrines of human nature and sin?

During World War II the United States pioneered a very different policy regarding the treatment of prisoners. The developer of the policy and the writer of the 1943 report describing its normative practice was Marine Maj. Sherwood F. Moran. His report, I am told, is still the most important document ever written on the interrogation of prisoners in warfare. Space permits only several of his important themes: (1) do not treat prisoners as enemy soldiers; for them the war is over; (2) do not assume that the prisoner in front of you probably possesses the enemy's deepest secrets; assume they will know a little, and if you interview enough prisoners who know a little, you will be able to identify and connect a lot of dots and assemble a better picture than you had before; (3) approach, and relate to, prisoners with as much understanding as you can, including understanding of their culture and language; and (4) treat prisoners humanely and with kindness.

How did such naïve idealism become, until 2003, the nearest thing to orthodoxy within American military culture? Moran's report was based upon research; humane interrogation methods were demonstrably more effective than the more macho approaches. From what background did Sherwood Moran frame this research and its important conclusions? He had been a career Christian missionary in Japan. His report was, and is, a serious expression of applied Christian ethics for warfare.[17]

In the late summer of 2005, three Republican senators—John Warner, Lindsey Graham, and John McCain, each a veteran and each serving on the Senate Armed Services Committee—proposed legislation that would outlaw cruel, inhumane, or degrading treatment of prisoners. As this is written, the administration is stonewalling this legislation—on the grounds that we are not dealing with "prisoners of war," but with "terrorists." Senator McCain replied that the essential, and inescapable, question is not "about who they are. It's about who we are." Why aren't some public evangelicals supporting this proposal? They could make the difference.

———

Or, take a less obvious example than war: a faithful people's relationship to nature. Few public evangelicals, in recent years, have made anything at all of God's assignment to us in Genesis to be "stewards" of God's creation. (I have sometimes wanted to ask them what there is in that assignment that they do not understand.) Let's get specific. While shopping in a "Christian" bookstore recently, an issue of *The Christian Sportsman* magazine caught my eye. Most of the articles featured the glories and methods of hunting and killing animals in the name of "sport"; several articles told inspiring or amusing stories from the shared experiences of buddies who went hunting together; at least one moose hunting venture was preceded each morning with a group devotional. Now, Jesus taught that the birds and animals matter to God, that God is affected when even one sparrow falls to the earth. IF we still ask, "What would Jesus do?" is it possible to infer from what he taught us that he would relish focusing a laser scope on Smoky the Bear (or strip-mining Mount Rushmore or dumping toxic waste in Lake Michigan)? Alas, no writer in *The Christian Sportsman* seemed to perceive any incompatibility between Scripture and sport killing. *The Christian Sportsman* simply assumes that sport hunting is one area of life for which the New Testament's ethical vision is irrelevant.

Many public evangelicals operate with an astonishingly truncated understanding of the gospel's ethic. To live as Christians is essentially defined as attending worship, having a daily devotional, living a clean life, affirming family values, saving souls— locally and globally—and supporting Republican policies.[18]

———

The syndicated columnist Cal Thomas apparently writes with the affirmation of all public evangelicals. In a 2005 column,[19] he rebuked the National Association of Evangelicals when its annual meeting expressed a concern for global warming and the earth's future health. Thomas quoted one of NAE's leaders, Rev. Rich Cizik, as saying, "I don't think God is going to ask us how he created the earth, but he will ask us what we did with what he created." In an attempt at refutation, Thomas claimed that Cizik had no biblical grounds for his view of creation. Thomas then declared, "There is no biblical expectation that a 'fallen' world can, should or will be improved before the return" of Christ. Evangelicals, he says, should stick to their "paramount calling," which he defines as working for the conversion of people at home and abroad.

Let me respond to Cal Thomas's claim in five ways. First, Cal Thomas does *not* tell evangelicals to quit trying to improve the world when he observes them working for social causes that he affirms; he gave NAE some *selective* advice.

Second, the world has in fact improved from time to time, through human effort, especially through the organized sustained efforts of Christians. In the eighteenth and nineteenth centuries, our evangelical predecessors helped rid much of the world of the slave trade, and then of slavery; according to Mr. Thomas, the biblical writers would not have known that such was possible. (A range of other "improvements" comes to mind, from the hundreds of millions who have gained literacy, education, health care, and freedom, to the widespread advance of civil rights, human rights, and religious rights, and the dismantling of apartheid, the Berlin Wall and Soviet Communism—all through sustained human effort, with the strong involvement of many evangelical Christians.)

Third, Mr. Thomas's contentions illustrate one of the most embarrassing facts about much of contemporary evangelical Christianity. Because of dynamics that we will explore later, "biblical" evangelical Christians, who assume that all of their views on all matters are "biblical," may not know what their Bible actually teaches. For example, a very useful book, *The Externally*

Focused Church,[20] encourages evangelical churches and their leaders to love and serve their communities, in part to build bridges to the pre-Christian people of their communities. The book includes a four-page appendix, reprinting *some* of the Bible verses that reveal "God's Heart for the Poor, the Needy, Widows, Orphans, and Aliens." Why was it necessary to include such verses in an appendix? Because too many "biblical Christians" no longer know what their Bible teaches on such matters.

Fourth, Mr. Thomas appears to be oblivious to the noble evangelical tradition that has often perceived a profound relationship between people's life condition and their receptivity to Christianity's gospel. For instance, there is no greater evangelical icon than C. H. Spurgeon, the late nineteenth-century English Baptist preacher. In his famous lecture "Obstacles to Soulwinning," Spurgeon reported his observations—from London, to England's rural areas, to Jamaica—that when people lack adequate jobs and economic hope, they are much less likely to respond to salvation's offer, or even to be spiritually interested. In such areas, he said, "indifference prevails."[21] Spurgeon also observed a connection between housing and Christianity's outreach. When working men live in crowded housing, they are much more likely to escape to the local tavern, where their company leads them in tragic directions. "You cannot hope," Spurgeon declared, "to be the means of saving men while they go to such places and meet with the company that is found there."[22] If Spurgeon was right, evangelicals who believe in reaching people for Christ have a serious stake in political and economic issues like good jobs and good housing for pre-Christian people.

Fifth, Mr. Thomas contends that evangelism and mission constitute God's "paramount calling" for evangelical Christians. I substantially agree. Indeed, this book is written to encourage and coach evangelicals to love and engage Democrats (and Republicans and others) with the gospel and its possibility for their lives; chapter 10 is devoted to practical perspectives and guidelines. Three insights, however, need to surface now: (1) we will not be credible to pre-Christian people if we do not know what our Scriptures actually teach about matters important to them; (2) they will not respond to us, and our invitations, if we are not involved with them in the real world, identifying with their pain, injustices, and ideals where we can, working for the kind of world that God wants; and (3) as my Asbury colleague Bob Tuttle would remind Mr. Thomas, we do not love people in order to evangelize them; we evangelize them because we love them.

No serious reflection on Jesus' ethic should omit his challenge to human hypocrisy, in all of its forms; he is very clear that we should tell the truth, mean what we say, and act consistently with our beliefs; especially, we should not obsess over "the speck of sawdust" in our brother's eye while ignoring the "plank" in our own eye (Matt. 7:3-5 NIV). The public's wide disillusionment with evangelical Christianity has reached the greatest consensus regarding its (perceived) hypocrisy.

Sometimes, the people perceive us, and the people we elect and support, as saying one thing while doing another. For instance:

- While the administration encourages millions of loyal-ists to display "Support Our Troops" ribbon symbols on their cars, the administration itself (two years into the Iraq war) still has not supported our troops with suffi-cient body armor, or vehicular armor, or a consistent set of reasons for being there, while reducing the health benefits of veterans and (as this is written) refusing to promise support to troops disabled in Iraq or Afghanistan. No public evangelical has pointed out even an apparent inconsistency. Moreover, since any war in the future will involve troops who should be supported, many evangelicals now seem precommitted to support *any* future war, waged for any reason.

- From Nixon on, every Republican president has campaigned promising smaller deficits and smaller government and has then delivered larger deficits and a larger
government, with no publicly reported complaints
from the public evangelicals.
- When the public evangelicals condemn "activist" judges
and Supreme Court justices, and they assure us that the
country would be better off with Republican-appointed
jurists, informed people know that Republican-
appointed judges already predominate on ten of the thirteen federal appellate courts, and seven of the nine
Supreme Court justices were appointed by Republican
presidents. Informed people noticed that, in the 2000
presidential election, when the Supreme Court (by a five
to four vote) stopped the vote recount in Florida and
thereby delivered the presidency to Mr. Bush, no public
evangelicals condemned the justices for being "activist."
- In the late 1990s, people heard the public evangelicals
denounce Mr. Clinton's immoral fling as a destructive
example to the moral sensitivities of America's youth.
Then people noticed that the public evangelicals
ignored greater moral failures to the right of center,
from Newt Gingrich and Robert Livingston to Rush
Limbaugh and Bill O'Reilly to Strom Thurmond and
Arnold Schwarzenegger to "Scooter" Libby and Tom
DeLay to Bill Frist and "Duke" Cunningham and others—much like their predecessors once ignored the
sins of J. Edgar Hoover, Joseph McCarthy, and Richard
Nixon. What keeps us from perceiving that the rancid
rope extending from (Spiro) Agnew through (Jack)
Abramoff is a cosmic embarrassment?
- The nation heard Vice President Cheney (in 2004) use
an egregious obscenity to Senator Leahy on the Senate
floor and Mrs. Bush's (2005) risqué stand-up bit, at a
banquet with journalists, about an (imaginary) visit to
Chippendales. The public evangelicals expressed no
moral indignation. Would they have been as silent if,

in 1999, Al Gore and Hillary Clinton had said the same things?

- In the 2004 debate between vice presidential candidates, the nation heard Mr. Cheney claim that Senator John Edwards had been away from the Senate campaigning for president so much that Cheney (who presides over the Senate) had never even met Edwards before they now met for the debate. When numerous photographs and videos later surfaced, showing the two men together, inside and outside the Senate, the possibility that Cheney was "'bearing false witness" did not seem to occur to the public evangelicals.

- In the 2004 election, Republicans (including Bush and Cheney) warned the people that John Edwards lacked sufficient experience in government to qualify for the vice presidency, but Edwards's six years in the senate was as long as Mr. Bush's prior state government experience when he sought the presidency and, in the 2000 election, Republicans commended him as "fully qualified" for the presidency.

- In the 2004 election, a Republican rumor campaign criticized how John Edwards made his money. (He'd been a successful trial lawyer in North Carolina and won several large class action lawsuits against large drug companies—which, as it happens, are large contributors to Republican campaigns.) The rumor campaign neglected to mention how Mr. Bush made his money.[23]

- In the 2004 presidential election, when the "Swift Boat Veterans for Truth" promoted the campaigns of the president and vice president, who had both dodged serving in the Vietnam War, by trashing the opposing candidate who had served in Vietnam (honorably, even heroically), no public evangelical spoke against this public indecency.

When public evangelicals are confronted with such incidents of apparent hypocrisy, they typically reply that "Some of the Democrats do it," or "That is the way in Washington," or "That's the way the world works," or "Everyone does it." Some of the Democrats, or the fringe movements that align with them (or against Republicans) have indeed engaged in similar practices. Several 1964 campaign commercials against Senator Barry Goldwater, for instance, were obscenely inaccurate, and several tactics of the 1987 campaign against Robert Bork for Supreme Court justice were astonishingly below the belt. Michael Moore's 2004 film *Fahrenheit 9/11* may have won awards in the documentary film class, but it was more propaganda than documentary. Hounds of the extreme Left *and* Right distorted Chief Justice John Roberts's philosophy and record through attack commercials before his confirmation. Karl Rove, alias "Bush's Brain," is widely acknowledged to have moved partisan campaigning to a new level of skill and sophistication, or (from another view) a new level of ruthlessness.[24]

My focus in this book, however, is not so much upon Democrats or Republicans as upon Christians, especially evangelical Christians. Jesus holds his followers to the standard of a higher righteousness. We are called to affirm, live by, and model the values and lifestyle of the kingdom of God. The ways of a fallen world may or may not work, but it is not the way the world was created to work and is called to work. "Everyone" does *not* do it that way, and Christians are not supposed to, and the world detects and detests the hypocrisy when we do. I suggest that, as in the case of methods for interrogating prisoners of war, a more Christian approach to political involvement, and campaigns, and toward candidates of the other party, would be a more effective way.

Of course, *if* we evangelical Christians got such a great social and political act together that we advanced justice, established world peace, educated the masses, and restored creation's health, *but* did not also help people experience second birth and God's purpose for their lives, we would leave them ultimately impoverished. We are especially called to fulfill the "apostolic" mission of the Christian movement. At our best, we have always known that Christ's church is an *ecclesia*—we are the "called out" people of God, and we are an *apostolate*—the sent out people of God. The God of Abraham still wants to bless the earth's peoples so we, the New Israel, have been called to be fishers of men and women, to go and make disciples among all peoples, to serve as ambassadors for Christ—through whom our reconciling Lord makes his appeal to others.

In the current political climate, this mission is also in jeopardy. Recent surveys show that, compared to a quarter century ago, a growing majority of people who profess Christian faith and attend churches are also people who support the Republican Party and a growing majority of people who do not profess faith or attend church support the Democratic Party. (If a majority of African American evangelicals did not still support the Democrats, this shift over the last quarter century would be even greater.)

The usual evangelical response to the growing number of nonbelieving Democrats could not be more pathological. Consider two points. One is that many evangelical leaders have grossly misperceived the main cause of this disparity. The most important single reason why fewer Democrats believe is because we evangelicals have not reached them. (Surely we did not fantasize that, if we abandoned them, the more liberal churches would reach them!) The data that show a net decline in church membership in the last three decades can be sliced at least several different ways, but one way suggests that our churches have substantially lost a generation of people who align with the Democratic Party. The second is that many evangelical leaders have grossly misperceived what our response to this growing disparity should be; they *shun* Democrats (who have, one must suppose, committed the unpardonable sin). May I propose a counter suggestion? The trend toward more "secular Democrats" should not be a pretext for abandoning them but an occasion for greater outreach to them.

NOTES

1. The term "gospel" in the New Testament carries the basic meaning of "good news" or "glad tidings." The gospel is the early Christian movement's essential message to the wider world, the core content of the Christian revelation. The narrative accounts, by Matthew, Mark, Luke, and John, of the breakthrough of God's gospel in Jesus of Nazareth, the Messiah ("Christus" in Greek), also came to be called "Gospels."

2. The Jewish scribes did not claim original revelation or interpretation of God's will; they essentially quoted their teacher and his tradition for interpreting God's Law.

3. Most of Israel did not perceive Jesus as the Messiah; they expected a Davidic military king, but Jesus adopted Isaiah's model of a "Suffering Servant."

4. The Greek word for "Fish" (as transliterated "Ichthus" into our alphabet) served as an acronym, standing for "Jesus Christ, of God the Son, Savior."

5. "Grace" essentially carries the two meanings of "unmerited favor" and supernatural assistance.

6. God's "righteousness" refers to what God does to make the relationship right between God and people, and to make people right.

7. God's "agape," and the agape love we are called to live by, refers not so much to any feeling (like "compassion" does), but rather to God's good will toward people and toward the rest of creation.

8. This peace refers both to an absence of conflict and violence and, even more, to the presence of good will and community. Jesus is often said to have brought his peaceable kingdom.

9. Jesus employs this metaphor in John 3, referring to a second chance, a new beginning, and a new life for people—all of which comes from God through spiritual experience.

10. The gospel, especially in Paul's emphasis, emphasizes that the human condition is one of estrangement, or alienation, from God, from others, from ourselves, and from creation, but the atoning death of Christ made a restored relationship with God possible and with other people, ourselves, and creation.

11. The early Christians believed that Jesus' Incarnation and substitutionary death purchased our deliverance from the penalty and power of sin and restored us to communion with God.

12. Justification is a legal metaphor, meaning that people who are "in Christ" are declared righteous. Because we accept the death of Christ in our behalf, God "imputes" Christ's righteousness to us.

13. Salvation carried the dual sense of being rescued from our sins and being made whole in Christ. The term in the New Testament did not originally emphasize "going to heaven," which, for many professing Christians today is (mis)understood to be its only meaning.

14. Sanctification refers to a process or experience, subsequent to justification, in which Christ's righteousness is "imparted" within us, thereby liberating us from the power of sin and enabling us to live the life of Love and become the people we were meant to be.

15. Abundant life and eternal life are largely synonymous terms, as both refer to the quality of life people experience in a relationship with God. Abundant life did not originally include the meaning that the "prosperity gospel" evangelicals now attach to it; eternal life included the meaning that life in Christ continues beyond death.

16. In civilian life, surveys show U.S. people actually murder their fellow citizens at a higher rate than in any other industrial nation. If one replies that a disproportionate number of the nation's murders occur in certain ethnic and class populations, one should recall that a disproportionate number of our troops are recruited from those populations.

17. For more on Moran's perspective see Stephen Budiansky, "Truth Extraction: A classic text on interrogating enemy captives offers a counterintuitive lesson on the best way to get information," *The Atlantic*, vol. 295, number 5 (June 2005), 32-35.

18. In other words, the ethic of many evangelical Christians today is indistinguishable from the Mormon ethic.

19. Cal Thomas, "Evangelicals should focus on saving souls, not the planet," *The Lexington Herald Leader* (March 18, 2005), A15.

20. Rick Rusaw and Eric Swanson, *The Externally Focused Church* (Loveland, Colo.: Group, 2004).

21. C. H. Spurgeon, *The Soulwinner* (Boston: Whitaker House, 1995), 105-106.

22. Ibid., 114.

23. In 1989, when his father was president, Mr. Bush bought a 2 percent share in the Texas Rangers baseball team for $500,000; the other partners soon increased (as a gift) his equity to $2,000,000. He persuaded the city of Arlington to build a new $190,000,000 stadium that, at taxpayer expense, increased the market value of the team. In 1994, Bush sold his share for $15,000,000.

24. Joshua Green researched the history and range of Rove's career as a campaign leader, including some relatively obscure campaigns in Texas and other states. Green tells an engaging story in "Karl Rove in a Corner," in the November 2004 issue of *The Atlantic Monthly*.

CHAPTER FOUR

THE (SUB-CHRISTIAN) HISTORY OF CHRISTIANITY'S STEWARDSHIP OF ITS GOSPEL AND ETHIC

How did it come to this? How did it happen that many of the evangelical churches in our ideologically polarized nation gave up on, wrote off, and seem inclined to demonize about half of the nation's people called "Democrats"? What we are experiencing is but the latest chapter in a very long struggle that has a serious history.

Christianity's history has some important precedents in the history of the Hebrew people. The God of Abraham had raised up Israel to be his means for blessing the other peoples of the earth. Israel's God wanted to deploy Israel in a mission to take "light for the Gentiles," (Isa. 49:6 NIV) that the salvation of Israel's God might extend to the whole inhabited planet. This mission was supposed to extend even to peoples like the Ninevites, who, in culture, beliefs, values, and lifestyle were threateningly unlike that of the Israelites. Israel, however, persistently ignored its mission, usually withdrawing from other peoples into the myth of the nation's superiority as God's chosen people. By the last century B.C., however, Jewish synagogues began welcoming "proselytes"—Gentiles who had submitted to circumcision, given up pork, obeyed Sabbath laws, adopted Jewish customs, and had proven themselves willing to "go native" and become more Jewish than most of the good Jews were.

The very young Christian movement's first church was a network of house churches in Jerusalem, which tended to reproduce synagogue patterns in its life together. The Jerusalem church was, initially, a movement of fulfilled Jews who were deeply convinced that Jesus of Nazareth was Israel's promised Messiah, that God had validated this claim by raising him from death. They believed that this new expression of Abrahamic faith was entrusted to them for the sake of all peoples, so they invited receptive Gentiles. Continuing the synagogue pattern, the Jerusalem church welcomed Gentiles into their fellowships IF they submitted to circumcision, etc. To become a Christian, they assumed, included becoming culturally kosher. The Jerusalem church probably worshiped in Aramaic (the folk version of Hebrew, used in Galilee and elsewhere, that Jesus spoke), so becoming a disciple probably involved learning the language of the church people. The Jerusalem church almost certainly expected all members to share their political views about the Roman occupation! Furthermore, as the Jesus Movement spread, the Jerusalem church thought of itself as the movement's headquarters.

The "headquarters" church became provoked when, up north in Antioch, Gentiles were becoming disciples of Jesus without becoming culturally Jewish. The Jerusalem church did what "headquarters" has usually done ever since. They sent a "consultant" to Antioch to enforce Jerusalem's policies upon the young movement in Antioch. They delegated this assignment to Barnabas who, granting their agenda, was a counterproductive choice. Why? Luke tells us that Barnabas was "a good man, full of the Holy Spirit" (Acts 11:24). So he was not a typical consultant. He approached the movement in Antioch with openness, saw what God was doing, and wrote back to Jerusalem that he liked what he saw. Headquarters was infuriated.

So Jerusalem then did what almost any headquarters would do: they called a meeting. That meeting (called "The Jerusalem Council" in the Christian tradition) is reported in Acts 15. Three parties assembled. The "Judaizers," led by James (the Lord's brother and leader of the Jerusalem church), believed that Gentiles who wanted to be Jesus-followers must adopt culturally Jewish ways. The "Indigenizers," led by Paul, could not have disagreed more; they believed that the young movement was called to adapt to every tongue and culture in the known world. So the Judaizers said to the world, "You adopt our culture," and the Indigenizers said to the world, "We will adapt to your culture." Simon Peter led the third team (which I am tempted to name the "Compromisers"). Peter started close to James's position but moved toward Paul's. When he cast his considerable weight with the Indigenizers, Paul's team won! The Christian movement's official policy now meant that the peoples of the known world did not have to become like the people already in the church, culturally, as the price of becoming Christians. The Christian movement was now free to adapt to all the tongues and cultures of the earth. This principle of "indigenous Christianity" liberated the young movement to become the world's most universal faith.

———&&&——— ———&&&——— ———&&&———

Now, the theoretical issues involved in the relationship between Christianity and culture are too many and too sophisticated to do justice to here. Some theological explanation might be useful. Except for the "primal" (or "folk") religions that serve only one people—like, say, the Masai of East Africa or the Inuit of the Arctic, the principle of "indigeneity" is a radical idea for "world" religions. Most world religions (some more than others) are tied to the culture in which the religion emerged; the culture's religious meanings were lifted to normative religious status. Furthermore, some are tied to the original language as well. (Islam, for instance, is culturally Arabic. Muslims believe that the Koran cannot be translated adequately into any other language, so to become a Muslim means, in part, to become culturally Arabic and an Arabic Koran reader. By contrast, Christians believe that the Scriptures can be adequately translated into any language and that confidence has now catalyzed over two thousand indigenous translations.) Paul, however, presumably reflected upon Jesus' Incarnation, which involved his complete adaptation to the dialect and customs of Galilean peasant Jews; Paul concluded that, as the Body of Christ, we are called to express the gospel through this principle of Incarnation, everywhere. So Paul commended to the church his policy to "become all things to all people, that I might by all means save some" (1 Cor. 9:12-23).

Four terms can help us cut through some of the remaining fog: message, mission, style, and strategy. Christians who believe themselves to be in Paul's apostolic tradition believe that we must not change the *message*, because the gospel is not a mere human construction but has been revealed; this "faith which was once delivered unto the saints" (Jude 3 KJV) is the only thing we have to offer the human race that it doesn't already have![1] To communicate its meaning cross-culturally (and often from one generation to the next), however, usually involves adapting to a *style* that fits the target culture. Again, Christians in Paul's tradition have no interest in changing the *mission*, because our main business in the kingdom's service has been revealed and is not for us to decide. Effective mission *strategy*, however, will vary significantly from one context to another; mission necessarily looks different among a literate people than among a nonliterate people, different in an oppressive political context than in a freer context, different in an Arctic village than in a European city, etc.

The four terms can help us understand the contrasting points of view between the "Judaizers" and the "Indigenizers." The Judaizers, for instance, believed that the original style and strategy have to be retained everywhere lest the message and mission be compromised. Eastern Orthodoxy,[2] and other traditional approaches to Christianity, have also tended to freeze and perpetuate the message, mission, style, and strategy from their tradition's foundational period. Other options have emerged more recently. Liberal Christianity has tended to change the message and mission to be more in sync with the Enlightenment and modernity, while retaining the tradition's language and liturgical style. In more extreme expressions, many "new religious movements" (like Jehovah's Witnesses, the Latter Day Saints, and many others) have retained Christian symbols while changing their meaning. Other new religious movements have changed message, mission, style, AND strategy. Though oversimplified, the following table helps visualize the options:

	Same Message and Mission	*Different Message and Mission*
Same Style and Strategy	**Traditional Christianity**	**Liberal Christianity**
Different Style and Strategy	**Indigenous Christianity**	**New Religions**

If you would judge from the life and style of most churches in most times and places, you'd get the impression that the Judaizers prevailed in the meeting reported in Acts 15. This becomes apparent when you lift the Jerusalem church's point of view just one step up the ladder of abstraction: they were the first church in history to expect new Christians to be (or become) "like church people." My book *Radical Outreach*[3] contends that the Judaizing party has often changed clothing, and even the issues, over time, but its insistence that all the people that we will really accept as Christians must be "like us" culturally has prevailed more often than not. Two cases should demonstrate this.

The early apostles learned, from Jesus' own ministry to such diverse groups as lepers, blind people, deaf people, and possessed people, and to tax collectors, and even zealots (first-century terrorists), that all people mattered to God and it was possible to reach all types of people. Most of the original apostles planted

Christianity among "barbarian" peoples; several even reached cannibal peoples. This daring apostolic tradition, however, was rapidly lost. By the late second century (if not earlier), the church assumed that people had to be sufficiently "civilized" to be "Christianized." Following Constantine's "conversion," the Establishment Christianity of the Roman Empire assumed for two hundred years that, by definition, it was not possible for "barbarians" to become Christians. As I explain in *The Celtic Way of Evangelism*,[4] it took Patrick's evangelization of the Irish to demonstrate that the "impossible" had been possible all along.

John Wesley faced a version of this same pathology in the eighteenth-century Church of England. As "common people" were pushed out of the countryside by the closure of formerly open lands and were pulled into the cities by the jobs now promised by the Industrial Revolution, the urban churches of the Church of England never shifted into any notable mission or outreach to include these newer urban people in the life of the churches. Why? For no more profound reason than this: the new people were not like the genteel members of the parish churches. Church leaders seem to have reasoned like this: "How could these new people become Christians? If they did come to church, they would not know when to stand up, when to sit down, or when to kneel. The clothes they wear are not fit for church. They have never acquired a church etiquette, they cannot afford to rent a pew, and they do not read well enough to navigate the Book of Common Prayer. How could such people become Christians?"

John Wesley and his eighteenth-century Methodists raised up a powerful, contagious, and redemptive movement from among the very populations that allegedly could not be Christianized. When Wesley was asked what made his Methodism different from the polite, proper, and powerless conventional religion of his land, he explained[5] that in the Methodist movement,

> The drunkard commenced sober and temperate. The whore-monger abstained from adultery and fornication, the unjust from oppression and wrong. He that had been accustomed to

36

curse and swear now swore no more. The sluggard began to work. The miser learned to deal his bread for the hungry and to cover the naked with a garment. Indeed the whole form of their life was changed.

I am suggesting that, in the last quarter century, we have experienced another chapter in this tragic volume—this one written by American evangelicals. Tens of thousands of churches in the United States have circled the wagons in self-protection against the secular world. Their churches are no longer "hospitals for sinners," but closed shops for the saints—defined as the people who "belong to us" IF they believe, behave, and ballot "like us." While they have retained the "evangelical" label for themselves, they seem to regard Wesley as wrong at two points: (1) "Unjust" people no longer need to "abstain" from "oppression and wrong." (2) Since the "misers" have obviously been blessed by God and overtaxed by the federal government, they are "entitled" to keep more money for themselves and to ignore the hungry and naked. In many of these churches, Democrats are now perceived as the new lepers. Since statistics show that fewer Democrats now profess faith and attend church than Republicans, this "proves," they say, that "Democrat-types" are hopeless.

I am suggesting that it is possible, and more faithful, to interpret the data another way. I am a longtime student, denominational executive, dean, and professor in Christian mission and evangelism. From such a vocational perspective, I propose that because evangelicals substantially abandoned the Democratic Party and its people a quarter century ago, it was entirely predictable that, in time, fewer Democrats would be Christian believers. Since we were entrusted with the gospel for the sake of other people, and since we once abandoned the Democrats who are now less likely to believe, then the judgment of the Lord may be more upon us than upon them, and there are compelling reasons for us to repent and change our ways.

I propose that we are called in our apostolic mission to love, serve, witness, and make disciples in every population sector (including both of the major parties and the smaller special interest parties) and to join in any and all common causes that help move society, or the world, more toward God's revealed purposes. Furthermore, both major parties need more people who are ambassadors for Christ *first*, who "know better" than to be co-opted by any ideological wing of a political party. This would mean the recovery of a compassionate mission, church by church, in every community, to Democrats and with Democrats, as well as Republicans.

In other words, Christianity has a long and nasty habit of writing off one population after another as hopeless; the evangelical abdication of the people called "Democrats" is the latest major case. However, our (more-or-less unconscious) involvement in this pattern begs two important questions: *How* does that happen? *Why* do Christians repeatedly view whole populations through lenses that block our vision of what they can become by God's grace? The next chapter explains that the problem emerges through "social influence."

NOTES

1. The gospel's communicators, of course, must live in a fresh conversation with the Scriptures to understand the gospel with greater precision and nuanced understanding; too many of its would-be communicators assume that their forbears, in their ecclesiastical tradition, got it right, so we don't really have to think about it any more! Furthermore, the gospel's meaningful communication to each culture, and rising generation, mandates more imagination than most communicators devote to it.

2. Eastern Orthodoxy had some early and notable exceptions, such as the mission of Methodius and Cyril in reaching several Slavic peoples, but Eastern Orthodoxy has not been a serious cross-cultural mission movement for most of the last millennium.

3. George G. Hunter III, *Radical Outreach: The Recovery of Apostolic Ministry and Evangelism* (Nashville: Abingdon Press, 2003).

4. George G. Hunter III, *The Celtic Way of Evangelism: How Christianity Can Reach the West . . . Again* (Nashville: Abingdon Press, 2000).

5. Stanley Ayling, *John Wesley* (Nashville: Abingdon Press, 1982), 158.

CHAPTER FIVE

"SOCIAL INFLUENCE" AND CHRISTIAN BELIEF TODAY

So far, we have seen that American evangelical Christianity often has not represented the full biblical message and ethic, nor its vision to "disciple" ALL of the earth's peoples. We often *assume* that "our tradition" represents something like the standard for full faithfulness, while actually featuring only a few of the gospel's many themes. We often wish that other traditions were engaged in "apostolic mission" as we are, while we ignore many peoples the apostles would reach. Our vision of the kind of world that we believe God wants is often the equivalent of a one- or two-string guitar, but we are so confident we've got it right, and our priorities are God's, that we neglect to consult the Book. While our "sins" undoubtedly account for some of this, the sheer power of "social influence" upon what we believe and how we see the world is a subtle but pervasive force upon us. Leaders who are oblivious to social influence continue to be its victims—like corks pushed by every wave in the sea, but leaders who are aware of it can transcend it, and even see (and define) reality more clearly. We can most easily observe the power of social influence in a case such as the following.

Donald McGavran, the late mission statesman, recalled an incident from his father's missionary career in India.[1] John McGavran visited a village where the people, to his knowledge, had little or no prior contact with Christians. He set up camp and, feeling hungry, he shot three ducks in the nearby lake. He said to the village people who had gathered that if someone would swim out and fetch the ducks, he would pay. They expressed reluctance because they believed that a god inhabited the lake; the god pulled people under and they died. McGavran reasoned that if *he* swam out for the ducks and survived, "this will destroy their belief in that god." As he swam, he felt weeds and vines within a foot of the surface, so he swam as near to the surface as possible, and as he pushed the ducks to the shore, he expected the village to be liberated from their belief in the lake-god. What happened when he emerged from the water? "The outcome was not what he expected. Instead of joyfully declaring, 'There is no god there,' they immediately said, 'This man is a god himself. He's a bigger god than the other. He has more power.'" Before he discovered the people's new theological conclusion and could dissuade them from it, "they brought a chicken from the village and sacrificed it to him!"

This case, unique only in the specifics, is a window into how human groups and societies reach conclusions, see their world, and live out their life in community. We tend to see the world the way our peers do. When something happens that we do not understand, we talk with each other, we connect the dots that we can see, we combine that perception with what we already "know," and then we "frame" the event to fit our worldview. Together, we socially construct our perception of reality.

We can observe this social principle reflected in Scripture. In John 9, for instance, Jesus and his disciples engaged "a man blind from birth." Jesus' disciples asked him, "Rabbi, who sinned, this man or his parents, that he was born blind?" In Galilean culture, the people had agreed on two possible causes for the mystery of blindness—the blind person's sins or the sins of his parents.

Jesus answered that *neither* of the (socially) known possible causes of blindness accounted for this man's blindness. (Notice the revolutionary insight behind his answer: Jesus' disciples can sometimes misunderstand a problem's cause and can see the world inaccurately.)

While for centuries some thinkers have had some knowledge of social influence and how it creates shared perceptions, twentieth-century research in social psychology advanced our knowledge of this phenomenon dramatically. Following World War II, some scholars observed how people are influenced by others, even against their better judgment; they observed people often changing their perceptions, beliefs, and behaviors to conform to their group.

Solomon Asch led several studies in the 1950s that demonstrated group influence upon individuals' perceptions. In one study, an unsuspecting experimental subject was placed in a group with three other people who were in collusion with the experimenter. The group would observe two white cards; the left card had a single vertical line, the right card featured three vertical lines of different lengths. The group's task was to identify which of the three lines on the right card was identical in length to the single line on the left card. In some groups, the experimenter's confederates were instructed to agree on an objectively false answer, to see what the experimental subject's response would be. Over 75 percent of these subjects "agreed" with the majority. (So great is the group's subtle power on individual perception, that some of the subjects reported in later interviews that they really did see the lines the way the others did, and some of the subjects who disagreed with the majority felt that they were probably wrong!) Even in the versions of the experiment in which the left line was much longer (ten inches) than the "correct" line on the right card (three inches), some subjects reported seeing what the majority said they saw. Many later studies have demonstrated that the influence of a group of people whom we know affects our perceptions more than the influence of a group of strangers, and our group's influence upon our attitudes, beliefs, and values is greater than its influence upon our visual perceptions,

especially over time. Furthermore, we now know that the influence of our culture, reference group, peer group, and immediate
contacts upon how most of us perceive the world is massive. So,
all members of the tribe on the day of John McGavran's swim
"saw" the same "god."

While Solomon Asch studied group effects upon individual
perception, protégé Stanley Milgram studied the effects of group
expectations for people and the effects of authority upon individual behavior. In his most famous experiment, subjects were
told they were needed to administer electric shock "punish-
ments" to people in an adjacent room—who pretended to scream
when the subject pushed the button. Some 65 percent of
Milgram's adult male subjects complied with the expectations of
the research leader and the control group. Milgram contended
that dynamics such as these could help explain the Holocaust;
behavioral scientists often cite such research to explain the abuse
of prisoners of war. So, the tribal members on the day of John
McGavran's swim "saw" the new "god" their peers expected them
to see.

Behavioral scientists have discovered that different people
play different roles in their community's perceptions and actions.
Some people, in every social group, are "opinion leaders." They
embody the group's beliefs and values, their judgment is widely
trusted, and when they take the initiative in connecting the
dots, the group is much more likely to accept their perception
than if a socially marginal person ventures the same conclusion.
The gathering that welcomed John McGavran as a deity
was, undoubtedly, led to the conclusion by two or three opinion
leaders.

Behavioral scientists have also discovered that almost every
person has a few people in his or her life who serve as "significant
others." We especially tend to believe what our significant others
tell us about the world. (Or, if we have an "oppositional disorder,"
we see the world in a way that opposes our significant other's
view.) We especially tend to see *ourselves* the way our significant
others see us (or the way we think they see us). Almost every person we meet has a self-image and a self-understanding that has

been profoundly affected by how significant others see, or how they think they see, him or her. So, the saying goes, "I am not who I think I am, I am not who you think I am, I am who I think you think I am." When, as John McGavran swam toward the shore, and the gathered tribesmen heard some opinion leader say, "He's a god, greater than the lake god," many would have checked the face of a significant other to see if that person agreed.

The dynamics of social influence are by no means confined to local settings and interpersonal relations. The tribesmen in that Indian village were part of a much larger society with its own distinctive "culture." A people will, through social influence and over extended time, develop their own set of attitudes, beliefs, values, and customs—which then shape how the people think and much of what they do. Through "socialization," they pass on that culture to the next generation and the next. Some of a culture's beliefs and values become "core"; those beliefs and values provide the people's "*worldview*," which functions like the "lens" through which they perceive reality. A culture's worldview typically includes core beliefs about nature (and how people should live in relation to nature), human nature (such as whether humans are rational or irrational, good or evil—and whether people can change), and the supernatural (involving issues like the meaning of human life and whether or not the cosmic order can be understood).

In other words, a culture develops its own *religious* worldview, or a "folk religion." When the people adopt a "higher religion" (such as Christianity), they typically combine symbols, assumptions, beliefs, and values of the new religion with the old; often, as in folk Roman Catholicism in Latin America, the blend involves attaching some of the new Christian symbols to the old religious meanings—while retaining the old meanings. American culture has, of course, developed its characteristic "folk religious" view. Nature, for instance, is there for us to use (or exploit), human beings can be reasonable, and people are good enough that you can "trust, but verify." American folk religion has *no* consensus on whether human beings can change. In relation to the supernatural, it is *very* important to avoid bad luck and get good luck on your side. Our folk religion (scholars often call it American civil religion) assumes that God is on our side. In the generation spanning the late nineteenth century and the early twentieth century, it was America's manifest destiny to win the West, and to expand the United States' influence, globally.

Once a group has connected the dots and assigned meaning to some event, the group members assume their interpretation is correct. Individuals may have residual doubts about conclusions they reach, but groups typically do not. "Group humility" may qualify as another oxymoron. Essentially the same dynamics form the driving perceptions, beliefs, and values that characterize the "culture" of a whole society. A culture, however, is even *more* likely than a group to assume that its view of reality is obviously correct. Unless people are educated into a cross-cultural perspective, groups ranging in size from a family or a gang, to a vocational association or a whole society, are afflicted with naïve realism—the way *we* see the world is the way it is. So, one society "knows" that blindness is symptomatic of a curse, another that it is caused by evil spirits, another that it is a virus, or germ, or birth defect, another that it is caused by the person's own sins, or those of his parents, another that the person's condition is a consequence of how he lived his previous life.

Furthermore, families, groups, teams, organizations, and societies *expect* their members to see the world like "we" do. While some groups, organizations, and societies permit some varied points of view within their ranks (and democracies are *supposed* to encourage diverse points of view), there is a limit; when individuals speak or behave beyond that limit, they are typically warned, marginalized, ostracized, excommunicated, or otherwise rejected by the group. So individuals in the tribal village would have experienced some pressure to agree that John McGavran was a god.

While it is natural for an association of people to share views that they expect any member to share if he or she is "one of us," social influence can become pathological (and, yes, "sinful"). Psychologist Irving Janis in 1972 labeled this pathology "Groupthink." When associations, ranging from teams to nations, strongly succumb to naïve realism, and when they are convinced of their own righteousness and invincibility, and when they value cohesiveness and unanimity so much that they *selectively* gather information, and when they ignore contrasting information, experts, and alternatives—that is the exact recipe for Groupthink. Janis and his protégés in the field of group communication concluded that such national tragedies as Pearl Harbor, the Bay of Pigs invasion, the Vietnam War, Watergate, and the Challenger space shuttle explosion were consequences of Groupthink.

More recently, the bipartisan Senate intelligence committee's investigation into the decision to launch the United States' war in Iraq concluded that Groupthink hijacked what should have been a more careful decision process. The administration "cherry picked" the available intelligence data to justify the war (which Bush and Cheney were interested in before 9/11), ignored other data and the many experts with contrasting judgments, and charged into war. (In Great Britain, the Butler Report demonstrated that similar dynamics drove the Blair administration in its rush to war as the United States' obligatory ally, though they found no pre-9/11 interest in invading Iraq.) So after Secretary of State Colin Powell failed to persuade many United Nations representatives to see Iraq "our way," and (as one joke suggested) with the substantial help of only three nations—England, the United Kingdom, and Great Britain—the United States initiated a "preemptive war" in Iraq for the following reasons: (1) Saddam Hussein was "behind 9/11"; (2) he played a major role in al-Qaida's agenda against the West; (3) he had "weapons of mass destruction" (chemical weapons and biological weapons); (4) he planned to build and deploy nuclear weapons; and (5) he was an imminent threat to Iraq's neighbors, the United States, and the world. The world now knows that such reasons were not valid, so the war's stated purpose has shifted several times—to objectives ranging from eliminating Iraq's alleged "weapons-of-mass-destruction related program," to freeing Iraq, and to advancing freedom and democracy in the Middle East, and more broadly.[2]

The perspectives and behaviors that social influence and (especially) Groupthink produce in their people's minds can "stick," and they "script" their people to speak and act, on cue, almost ritualistically, for a very long time. The week I am writing this, "Deep Throat" has, after three decades, revealed his identity. Mark Felt, now 91, was deputy director of the FBI during the Richard Nixon presidency and has now identified himself as the legendary source for the Bob Woodward and Carl Bernstein Watergate stories in *The Washington Post*. The news-talk shows have brought much of this period back to memory, and I thought about how much has not changed in three decades. For instance:

- Conservative pundits from the Nixon era, like Patrick Buchanan, G. Gordon Liddy, and even Charles Colson quickly defined the Mark Felt issue as a "loyalty" issue. Mark Felt was *"disloyal"* to President Nixon and to the institution of the presidency, (presumably) even though he knew that the Republican National Committee had broken the law by breaking into the Democratic Party headquarters at the Watergate Hotel and that the White House was now committing crimes to cover up the Watergate crime, and that Attorney General John Mitchell's Justice department was politicized and corrupt, and that FBI Director Patrick Gray was undermining the Watergate investigation in the White House's behalf. The Bush administration today, if anything, values loyalty above all else; Bush expects his people to be loyal to him no matter what, and Bush is exceedingly loyal to his people who are loyal to him. When *any* of the several Bush administration people have left government service and have reported how policy is made in the Bush White House, an orchestrated chorus of spokespersons has risen to challenge their "loyalty."

  Do I need to point out that ultimate loyalty to *any* human being is *not* a supreme value in biblical Christianity, especially in comparison to the biblical values of truth and justice? Ultimate loyalty to anyone or anything, other than God and God's will, is *idolatry*. The public evangelicals have not critiqued the Republican loyalty-above-all ethic, perhaps because loyalty to the people in charge has become such a big deal in *some* of the most "evangelical" denominations and parachurch organizations and megachurches!

The Republican emphasis upon loyalty has deep roots, philosophically. The ideological father of some of the big ideas that now shape the Republican Party is no longer Abraham Lincoln, but Alexander Hamilton. Hamilton was a formidable mind, especially in finance; he was a leader of the Federalist Party and once served as Secretary of the Treasury. Philosophically, he believed that the federal government should serve and advance "the common good." He also believed, however, that the decisions for contributing to the common good should be made by the "talented few"— understood as male leaders drawn from the wealthy and aristocratic slice of society. They had the wisdom and foresight to know what was best for everyone, but the masses did not.

Hamilton was, after all, much more "European" than most of his American contemporaries, and much of Europe still believed in "the divine right" of kings and, to some degree, of the aristocracy. In time, Jeffersonian democracy overwhelmed the Federalist Party, which, in time, died as an organization. But its ideas never died; they have bobbed up and down in America's ancestral memory ever since. They surfaced again in the Eisenhower era, they became more central (if subconscious) in the Nixon administration, and more consciously central in the Reagan, Bush I, and (especially) Bush II administrations.

Today's secularized version of the old European doctrine of "the divine right" of kings takes the form of an "entitlement mentality." The Republican sense of an entitlement to rule, I submit, was behind the Nixon era expectation of supreme loyalty to the president (whether he was right or wrong, legal or illegal) and was behind the Republican rage that surfaced when Bill Clinton (from common roots) defeated patrician George H. W. Bush's bid for reelection. Entitlement was a driver behind their relentless investigation of Clinton and his impeachment—which was (as admitted in 2005 by retiring Republican Congressman Henry Hyde) also a retaliation for the Democrat-led impeachment process against Nixon that forced his resignation. Something like dynastic entitlement surfaced when, during the 2000 Florida vote recount, one Supreme Court justice said it would be "wrong" to deny Mr. Bush the presidency.

So loyalty, based on entitlement to rule, seems to be a prevailing Republican value; the extent of loyalty now expected toward a Republican president would once have been expected only toward monarchs. (I am told that some Republicans, and their churches, are now praying for future presidents who will perpetuate Bush's "legacy.")

In an MSNBC poll, some 23 percent of a sampling of U.S. citizens agreed that Mark Felt was not a hero but a "turncoat." (It would not take a much greater percentage of a society's people who devote excessive loyalty to a president to constitute the critical mass necessary to engineer a totalitarian society.)

- Patrick Buchanan also attacked Mark Felt's *motives* for serving as "Deep Throat." Mr. Felt *may* have hoped that Nixon would appoint him to succeed J. Edgar Hoover as director of the FBI, so Mr. Buchanan tells us that sour grapes drove Mark Felt into a vindictive payback vendetta against the president of the United States of America. Now, psychologists have learned that the knowledge of human motives is very elusive;

we are a mystery to ourselves, and the most skilled therapists say they seldom fully understand why some of their counselees do what they do. The consensus is that virtually anything we do is driven by multiple motives, and some of those motives are conscious, and some are subconscious. So, no one fully knows why anyone does something, but never mind human complexity. Buchanan and several other Republican spokespersons quickly assured the nation that when Mark Felt was cooperating with the Woodward and Bernstein investigation thirty years ago, he was doing so for the most reprehensible motives they can now imagine.

Republican ideological attacks upon "disloyal" people and other detractors are not limited to the evil motives that they impose upon the source of irritation, but they are usually *personal* attacks. In television interviews on May 31 and June 1, 2005, just after the revelation of Mr. Felt as Deep Throat, Charles Colson said that Felt was unprofessional and characterized his behavior as skullduggery. G. Gordon Liddy (a convicted felon, but nevertheless an icon of the religious Right) called into question the ethics of Mark Felt's actions. Several others criticized Felt's method, or they charged that he went about it the wrong way; but they failed to tell us how else he could have done it, in the conditions he faced, that would have brought justice. Actually, they never mentioned justice nor reflected any interest in the truth about the Watergate scandal.

The integrity of organizations, institutions, and societies requires, of course, that they remember their identity, their main business, their driving values, and their foundational ideas; this requires some limit to the range of ideas they are free to import. In the American Medical Association, for instance, all ideas are not accorded equal status; the AMA is more likely to continue accounting for epidemics by resorting to virus theory or germ theory than it is likely to shift to, say, an alternate theory about bad luck or a witch's curse.

Organizations over extended time, however, may not retain as much of their original genius as they think. I have already suggested that the Republican Party is not as much the party of Abraham Lincoln and Theodore Roosevelt as it thinks, and it is now more the party of Alexander Hamilton than it knows. Christian denominations can be at least as vulnerable as political parties. For proof, I need look no further than my own (oxymoronic) denomination, The United Methodist Church. Eighteenth-century Methodism was built upon, and became a contagious worldwide movement because of, John Wesley's apostolic vision and message and his vivid sense that a "People of One Book" could "reform the nation and spread scriptural holiness across the land." Often, in the history of denominations, a later generation of leaders will assume they "know better" than their more brilliant founder.

In Methodism's case the alleged improvements were imposed in the fifth or sixth generation, when some leaders (influencing each other) came up with the idea that newer perspectives and theologies were preferable to those of the movement's founder. No "new theology" since has had the sticking power of even one generation; too many of our "leaders" have flitted from one new theology to another to another. A majority of Methodists are now afflicted with something like amnesia; they have no living memory of what it means to be followers of Jesus Christ in the tradition of Wesley. The most liberal of our churches have become so "hypertolerant," and have imported so many non-Christian ideas into the life of the church, that they are now like mules—they are so compromised they are incapable of reproduction; they cannot even retain a majority of their own children into adult discipleship. United Methodism, like many mainline denominations, stands in desperate need of recovering something like classical Christianity and a complete understanding of, and confidence in, the richness of Christianity's gospel.

It would be inappropriate, however, to assume that all of the "evangelical" denominations do in fact represent classical

Christianity and the whole gospel. Indeed, many of the newer evangelical denominations and movements, like independent Baptists, Pentecostals, and others, were raised up more to recover a few themes that the more historic churches had forgotten than to represent the complete Christian faith. So, for instance, the Pentecostal movement demonstrated that God could be experienced powerfully and not just "believed in"; that *all* people can be reached, even the most marginalized, and are redeemable by God's power; and that all believers are gifted by the Holy Spirit, not merely to sit on the sidelines and cheer the pastor's ministry, but to engage in ministry and make a difference in people's lives. Several of the newer denominations and traditions have made such enormous contributions that I shudder to think where we would be without them. As one of many examples, they have produced virtually all of the new music that people in most other churches love to sing.

They do not, however, feature anything like the whole message and wisdom of Scripture. Historically, they have not even claimed to.[3] They were raised up in specific circumstances around two or three big ideas or to serve a neglected population. Some of them have not valued higher education. Many of the most influential evangelical pastors in America lack any serious theological education. In some places, thousands of people hang on the words of engaging pulpit personalities who have never read Augustine or Anselm, Calvin or Kierkegaard. My point, for now, is that they often inadequately represent (or even understand) Christianity's social vision; they have seldom connected the message of the prophets and the Sermon on the Mount with the political struggles of their times.

It's not that American evangelicals have no ethic, but it is astonishingly similar to the ethic of American folk religion; its themes are sometimes *more* derived from American cultural values than from the biblical revelation. For example, consider the "four-letter words" that are taboo in American folk piety; one who says them is "cussing," and "good Christians" don't say such things. While there are good reasons for speaking and writing clean language, most of the four-letter words are not prohibited in Scripture per se. They are prohibited in American folk piety, which (in our "Groupthink") we assume to be biblical Christianity. Sometimes, unless we study what the Bible actually says and means, the culture's Groupthink refracts the Bible's meaning to fit ours. So, for most evangelical Christians, the fourth commandment—"Thou shalt not take the name of the Lord thy God in vain"— no longer refers to promising or oath taking (as it originally meant) but to swearing or cussing.

Most American evangelicals have arrived (unconsciously) about where the Mormons arrived consciously—claiming a "later revelation" that looked a whole lot like the contextualized ethic that Protestants had developed for the challenges of nineteenth-century frontier towns. They are clear on the evils of alcohol, drugs, and tobacco, and on the places to stay out of, the people to stay away from, and the words that must not be spoken, and they are clear on "family values." On everything else they are essentially Republicans—without understanding the social influence dynamics that caused them to lose much of their social conscience.

Perhaps it is time for evangelical church leaders to rediscover the full evangelical social ethic of the Scriptures, to affirm and implement the relevance of Christian faith for every area of life and society, to declare that "The earth is the Lord's, and the fulness thereof" (Ps. 24:1 KJV) and to welcome Jesus' own vision of the kingdom of God back into the consciousness, and the conscience, of our churches. Do we want God's will to be "done, on earth as it is in Heaven" (Matt. 6:10)? If we do, faithfulness would involve actually *using* the influence many evangelicals have with the Republican Party and the Bush administration.

I recently read Anne Lamott's latest book, *Plan B: Further Thoughts on Faith*. Lamott is a wonderful, vulnerable imagineer and stylist who always gives me some useful perspective on living as a Christian, especially when life is hard. Lamott is not subtle. She believes that we now have a "paranoid, right wing government," that we will be at war in Iraq for a very long time, and it gets her depressed almost every day. She fears that the country's black and Hispanic kids will be the most damaged by the war period's deficit spending. She confesses that she was "angry that our country's leaders had bullied and bought their way into pre-emptive war." Lamott seems much more sure than I am, however, that "the White House . . . lied their way into taking our country to war."[4]

My experience, in many groups, organizations, and other societies, would suggest that Mr. Bush and Mr. Cheney probably did *not* knowingly bear false witness about Iraq's "weapons of mass destruction," etc. Why? When "we" have influenced each other, over time, the perceptions we construct together seem very real, unless major evidence or influences compel us to change our minds. Once, for instance, the Russian people believed in the truth and promise of Communism, and in every "five-year plan." Eventually, when they observed that *every* "five-year plan" failed, they abandoned Communist doctrine. Returning to the example of John McGavran's swim, on that day, the Indian village's people genuinely believed in McGavran's "divinity." In time, he was able to persuade them otherwise; no one in the village today would recall their grandparents reminiscing about the god who proved more powerful than the god of the lake.

The Groupthink form that social influence can take, however, is different. When a group's people influence each other, and when they experience the social bonding, the adrenalin rush, the cohesion, and the sense of group righteousness that characterizes Groupthink, and *some* data appear supportive, they genuinely believe in the truth of the conclusions they reach and the validity of the actions they take. Furthermore, they are more immune to changing their minds later than in less extreme cases of social influence. When, for instance, a close and cohesive religious sect predicts the end of the world on a certain date, and the end does not materialize on that date, they simply reinterpret the data; because of their faithfulness and righteousness, God spared the whole world. So, after two years into the war in Iraq, Vice President Cheney announced that he was still convinced that Saddam Hussein had weapons of mass destruction and was in cahoots with Osama bin Laden and, therefore, we were entirely right to carry our military response to 9/11 to both Afghanistan and Iraq.

If you have read this far, I know what some of you are thinking. "If we saw all of this *your* way, George Hunter, Saddam Hussein would still be in power, wouldn't he?"

No. If we had only invaded Afghanistan, which had broad international support (even in much of the Muslim world), and had *not* also waged war in Iraq, the Saddam Hussein who was behind 9/11, had stocked piles of chemical, biological, and nuclear weapons, and was an imminent threat to neighboring nations and to the world would *not* be in power to today. Because *that* Saddam Hussein turned out to be a fiction—socially constructed by some people who believed that their construction represented reality. Furthermore, *if* we had stayed fully focused in Afghanistan and not invaded Iraq, it is much more likely that Osama bin Laden would now be history, and al-Qaida nearly so, and the Taliban would have been vanquished and would not now be staging a comeback, and the terrorist factory that we catalyzed by invading Iraq would not today be multiplying terrorists faster than anyone can keep up with.

So, social influence theory explains much of how we reach conclusions and see the world as groups and societies, but it fails to explain how some of the ideas take on a life of their own, and when expressed through speeches and debates, slogans and commercials, pamphlets and propaganda, do so much to unite, energize, mobilize and divide people. A much more ancient field of knowledge helps account for that.

NOTES

1. Donald A. McGavran, *The Satnami Story: A Thrilling Drama of Religious Change* (William Carey Library, 1990), 27-28.

2. While American funds were needed for the war, we were assured that Iraq's oil revenue would fund the country's reconstruction. As this is written (November 2005) Iraq is still *importing* oil for its needs.

3. The denomination named the "Full Gospel Church" features only four of the many themes of the gospel.

4. Anne Lamott, *Plan B: Further Thoughts on Faith* (New York: Riverhead Books, 2005), 4.

CHAPTER SIX

THE PUBLIC
COMMUNICATION (AND
MIS-COMMUNICATION)
OF CHRISTIANITY TODAY

A ll of the people who buy this book for the purpose of reading some "Rhetorical Theory" could hold a convention in a Volkswagen. Most people associate *rhetoric* with flowery language, or bombastic oratory, or the freshman composition course they once sweated. Rhetoric has a much better pedigree than that. It is the study of how people use words (and other symbols) to transmit messages, communicate meaning, inform each other, and influence each other. More broadly, rhetoric is the study of effective speaking and writing in human affairs.

Some of the greatest minds, from Plato and Aristotle to Saint Augustine and Francis Bacon, have contributed to the body of theory that helps us make sense of the controversies of our time and helps us to be more effective communicators of ideas. Recent rhetorical theorists have amplified our understanding of rhetoric's importance by demonstrating the effectiveness of rhetoric's creative power. (They use the term "constitutive power." For instance, through messages over time, a man and a woman may "constitute" a marriage, statesmen may constitute a nation, and a core group may constitute a church.) I have placed this theme last in the four "perspectives" chapters because rhetoric helps us make sense of our political world and also because it has much to teach us about the effective communication of the gospel—to which a later chapter is devoted.

If we took rhetoric's first lesson seriously, it could change American politics profoundly for the better. Aristotle's *Rhetoric* emphasizes that, in human affairs, we do not take sides and contend with each other in issues where the truth can be known with something like scientific certainty. So, few people dispute whether or not two plus two equals four, or whether water freezes at 32 degrees Fahrenheit or whether the earth is flat or spherical, because certain knowledge is readily available. We only engage in persuasive activity around matters in which the truth cannot be known with certainty, in which we strive for the greatest *probability* that we can reach. So, for instance, we cannot now know for certain whether it would be best to buy or sell Lilly stock, or what candidate X would do if elected, or whether nation X has secretly developed chemical weapons, or the *exact* degree to which global warming is a threat, is caused by human activity, or is reversible by human intervention. On many complex matters in politics, economics, and religion, upon which nonexperts cannot know for sure (and even the experts may disagree), we look for *reasons* that will help us arrive at enough *probability* to act upon.

Aristotle's probability perspective has two important implications for Christians who get involved in the political world. (1) While the two major parties may compete with each other for the privilege of serving the people, the political process—from nominating and campaigning to legislating and implementing—is supposed to be, and needs to be, fundamentally a *cooperative* one; no one side or advocate is likely to know the whole truth with informed certainty, so we need to learn from each other and even encourage each other to catalyze our own best reflection. (2) Aristotle's "probability" perspective also provides us with grounds for serious suspicion whenever we hear a candidate or party that claims more certainty on complex matters than is available to mere mortals in this life.[1] Some public personalities often *feel* remarkably confident in the absolute truth of their folk wisdom, or their preferred ideology, or the conclusions of their Groupthink experience, but subjective confidence (or arrogance) is not the same thing as informed certainty. As one type of example, people driven by folk wisdom or ideology usually assume that a complex problem (such as, say, illiteracy, poverty, terrorism, or the spread of AIDS) has a single cause and can be fixed with a single intervention; informed people know that any complex problem has multiple causes, some of which may not yet be known, and multiple interventions may be required to improve a problem that may never be fully solved.[2]

Dr. Harry G. Frankfurt, a moral philosopher at Princeton University, recently published a short but serious study of a kind of speaking we seem to hear more than ever today. His *On Bullshit*[3] (hereafter I will refer to "BS," except when quoting) may be the first published reflection on a way of speaking that all of us have observed, and probably have engaged in. Frankfurt believes that BS is such a pervasive and insidious problem in human affairs that no synonymous term like humbug, or claptrap, or balderdash carries quite the same emotively serious meaning as BS (although I suggest that in British English "rubbish" comes close). Frankfurt distinguishes BS from lying because intentional misrepresentation is necessarily involved in lying; when a speaker engages in BS, however, he or she may not know the truth, or even care to know the truth, of the matter at hand. In BS, the speaker has a different agenda than truth-knowing, or truth-telling, or truth concealment. He or she intends to get elected, or advance an agenda, or buy time, or win appreciation, or gain rapport with a crowd through discourse that simulates the appearance of truth-claim. As Frankfurt states cogently, "The essence of bullshit is not that it is *false* but that it is *phony*."[4]

Frankfurt wonders, with many of us, why there seems to be so much more BS today than in other times. One cause, he states, is the greater expectation (as in interviews and on talk shows) that one speak "off the top" to questions that one has not first reflected upon, that may exceed one's knowledge, or about which one may even be entirely uninformed. Most people are reluctant to admit that they do not know, so they BS their way through the moment. I would add the observation that, in such a moment, people often draw upon their culture's folk wisdom—which they assume to be true. I would also add that many people appraise Christianity by the sense (or nonsense) that they hear from Christianity's spokespersons, and evangelical Christianity's public representatives seldom represent Christianity so badly as when they "wing it" on radio and television talk shows. (Pat Robertson's public recommendation in August 2005 on his *700 Club* television show that the U. S. government should assassinate a South American head of state serves as a perfect example. The spontaneous chatter reflected *no* prior thought.) Too often, their "off the top" remarks are much more scripted by their culture's folk religion than by serious Christianity, and any residual Christian meaning gets drowned in the platitudes. The problem is compounded when the speaker mistakes an impulse or an adrenaline rush for the Holy Spirit. (It is very important that public Christians engage people's questions, but it is also very important to admit it when we do not know something; nothing is wrong with saying "I don't know," or "Let me get back to you on that," or "Let me give you two fragments of insight." If you then do your homework on a question or topic for which you were insufficiently prepared, you will do better the next time it comes up.)

While Plato's writing predated Frankfurt's by twenty-four centuries, Plato's indictment of the "Sophists" of ancient Greece addresses "BS" from a deeper perspective. In *Gorgias*, Plato observed that many of the most influential public leaders, in fields ranging from politics to religion, were not substantially informed, but their popular influence vastly exceeded their knowledge. Plato featured an analogy to make his point. Put two speakers, a physician and a candy maker, on a stage to speak to an audience of children *or* to an audience of adults who think like children. The audience will usually prefer the candy maker's offer to the physician's. The candy maker is pandering to the people's surface tastes, and they buy his delicious candy—even though the candy will undermine their health. By comparison, the physician offers things like bitter-tasting medicine and even amputations; the people are not usually attracted to the physician's offer, even though it will bring greater health.

Plato believed, however, that a different approach to public influence was both possible and desirable—the way of the "rhetor." At the risk of some oversimplification, it is possible to represent Plato's distinction between the "Sophist" and the "Rhetor" as follows:

- The Sophist is ignorant of, or indifferent to, Truth; the Rhetor loves and serves Truth.
- The Sophist wants personal victory and success; the Rhetor wants to impart truth and persuade the audience.
- The Sophist seeks his own interests; the Rhetor serves the audience's best interests.
- The Sophist engages people's motives, which when fulfilled, make people worse; the Rhetor speaks to motives that make people better.
- The Sophist affirms, and works entirely within, the people's folk wisdom; the Rhetor understands the folk wisdom and may engage it and affirm some of it, but to lead people to greater Truth.

Plato acknowledged that the Sophists were clever leaders, but they often advanced their purposes by flattering the people's folk wisdom, or by pandering to the people's prejudices, or by engaging in deceitful reasoning. They were like lawyers who had mastered the dubious skill of making the weaker case appear to be the stronger.

Many scholars today believe that Plato was too hard on the Sophists, and it is true that his stereotyped view of them does not fit their best thinkers and teachers, such as Isocrates. I have no doubt, however, that politics and religion today have more than their fair share of "Sophists" who do fit Plato's stereotype. Some of today's most influential religious leaders essentially attach Christian symbols to American folk religion; Jesus is (mis)represented as "SuperWASP," and the Christian lifestyle is indistinguishable from the American way of life. Many of America's most influential religious leaders have never done theological studies; of those, some compensate through serious lifetime study, but some do not. The latter are like the "doctor" who skipped medical school but still dispenses medicine—the medicine that people want. Some religious leaders offer only part of the gospel—the part that is the easiest part to accept, and they pass that part off as though it were the whole. Some religious leaders who did experience a theological education attended institutions where Christian ethics is not featured in the curriculum, so they may be clear on the gospel for individuals, but are thin representatives of the wider will of God. (The examples of transparent sophistry in American political speaking, especially in campaigns, are too numerous and too obvious to belabor here.)

In his later work, *Phaedrus*, Plato sketched ways in which advocates for truth (like the physician) could be more effective in their *de facto* competition with the Sophists' BS. He defined a true rhetoric as "the art of influencing the soul through words." He called for the rise of philosopher-advocates who would first pay the price to discover the truth on the matter in question, who would also work to understand human nature and audiences, and to define terms, and speak the people's language, and organize the speech in ways they could follow. Unlike the Sophists, the true Rhetor's goal is the communication of transcendent knowledge, not merely the tribe's folk-beliefs.

Aristotle was Plato's protégé, but he appreciated the best of the Sophists' thought. The Sophists perceived that sometimes in human affairs, absolute truth might not be attainable, or communicable. Aristotle arrived at his doctrine of "probability" from his study of several Sophists. But, essentially, he stood on Plato's shoulders and fleshed out Plato's suggestions of what a rhetorical theory in truth's service would look like. Aristotle said in *Rhetoric* that the speaker who pays the price to know the truth has an advantage "because truth and justice are by nature more powerful than their opposites." The effective public communication of truth requires, however, the assistance of the art of Rhetoric. So if we know the truth and lose, we have only ourselves to blame; we had the truth on our side, but neglected to learn the art of making truth publicly available. Aristotle taught that a speech takes place in a (social, historical, cultural, and immediate) context, and his *Rhetoric* devotes serious attention to audience analysis and the importance of strategically adapting to the audience.

Aristotle's model of the communication process—that communication takes place in an interaction between a speaker, a message, and an audience—has served us for twenty-three centuries. More specifically, he taught that persuasion takes place as a result of the *logos* of the message, the *pathos* of the audience, and the ethos of the speaker. *Ethos* is the appeal based on the character of the speaker. By the *logos* of the message he was referring to the reasons and the evidence that would enable the audience to accept the speaker's truth-claim. In discussing the *pathos* of the audience, he was featuring the importance of engaging the target population's needs and motives and helping them to feel in ways that are productive to the response the speaker wants. (People respond differently, say, when they are experiencing fear than they do when they are feeling courageous.)

While much more could be written from rhetorical theory, a discussion of Aristotle's doctrine of *ethos* and its implications must conclude this part of our discussion. When Aristotle observed the advocates in the legislature and law courts of ancient Athens, he perceived that an audience's perceptions of an advocate strongly influenced their response to the advocate's message. They seemed to be asking questions, perhaps subconsciously, about the advocate. Perhaps from interviewing auditors, Aristotle came to understand that, to believe the speaker, the audience must become convinced that the speaker is (1) a person of intelligence or competence or authority who is in a position to know the truth of the matter; (2) a person of character (or trust-worthiness); and (3) a person speaking with good will toward the audience, not to gain personal advantage. Of the three "modes of proof" (*ethos, logos,* and *pathos*), Aristotle wrote in *Rhetoric* that he was *almost* convinced that *ethos* is the most potent of the three. Furthermore, he assumed that the three factors he identi-fied were *the* operating factors in a speaker's ethos. He claimed that a speaker thought to be informed, and a good person, and a person of good will "*necessarily* has the confidence of his readers."

Aristotle's analysis of *ethos* was not *quite* as exhaustive as he thought. For instance, rhetorical researchers have identified a *dynamism* factor in the speaker's ethos. Many auditors, if not all, need to experience the speaker as interesting or energizing.

Kenneth Burke, a twentieth-century rhetorical theorist, con-tended that *identification* is a powerful factor in the relationship between speaker and audience. When the people have a sense that the speaker deeply understands them or shares their beliefs, their background, their history, their experiences, or their aspira-tions, they are strongly inclined to believe what the speaker says. In extreme cases, many people will assign to a speaker (with whom they deeply identify) a greater infallibility than Roman Catholic doctrine has ever assigned to the Bishop of Rome when he is speaking ex cathedra.

We now know that *credibility* is also a powerful factor in the communicator's ethos. Helmut Thielicke, the German theolo-gian and preacher of a generation ago, used to contend that the credibility of Christians and the church is the most important variable in whether secular people find Christianity worth con-sidering. My interview research with secular people who have little-or-no Christian memory, a project now spanning several decades, has strongly confirmed Thielicke's point, which can now be sliced in four different ways: (1) Some people wonder whether we *believe* what we say we believe; (2) Some people do not doubt that we believe it; they wonder if we *live by* what we believe; (3) Some people do not doubt that we believe it, or live it; they wonder whether it makes much *difference;* (4) There is also a consistency-with-what-they-know factor. They may know only a little about Jesus—such as that he taught love, or believed in peace, or taught the Golden Rule. When they hear a Christian advocate, they (reasonably) expect the advocate to include, or be consistent with, whatever they already know.

Christians who enter human affairs with a knowledge of Aristotle's paradigm will not be astonished when they observe that many people's confidence in the (perceived) *ethos* of their favored leader inclines them to believe, and defend, anything the leader says. (We *might* not be astonished when some Christians even elevate their favored advocate to stardom—permitting us to observe the *ultimate* oxymoron—the "Christian celebrity"!) Nor will they be astonished when they see people making decisions out of strong feelings (or out of a socially influenced group decision) about the way things are or what should be done. *Ethos* and *pathos* are likely to influence every issue and almost every auditor, and Christians cannot change that (even if they want to). Often in short supply, or even "missing in action" in politics today, are *good reasons* for doing what is proposed. Effective organizations and societies make decisions based on good reasons; worthy advocates are obligated to discover and communicate good reasons for what they propose; responsible members and citizens are supposed to insist on good reasons. A deliberative body will often short-circuit Aristotle's *logos* unless some people are constantly asking for good reasons (and the *real* reasons). Christians will advance good politics—and win interest in the Christian faith—if they insist on reason-based decisions and policies.

Christians will also advance biblical Christianity's credibility when, in addressing issues, they briefly share the biblical value from which they engage in reason giving. Sometimes, a reasonable role will involve exposing the assumption behind another point of view, or the flimsy evidence, the red herring, the BS, the *ad hominem* attack, or some other fallacy that people sometimes serve up disguised as a reason. When we remember to engage in such discussions with diplomacy, with love for the other people, and with appropriate assertiveness without aggressiveness, we will find ourselves valued and sought-out partners in the political process.

NOTES

1. So, for instance, on the occasions when President Bush has declared what motivates the terrorists, I experience some difficulty because I know he is not a student of psychology's literature on motivation, nor of Arabic culture, nor of the Koran, nor of the distinctive social influence dynamics in Islamic fundamentalist culture.

2. So, knowing the multiple causation of all complex problems, I can infer that a single intervention like a regressive tax cut will not mend the United States' floundering economy, and the imposing of national testing will not resolve education's struggles.

3. Harry G. Frankfurt, *On Bullshit* (Princeton, N.J.: Princeton University Press, 2005).

4. Frankfurt, *On Bullshit*, 47. The week before I wrote this, Karl Rove—the strategist for Bush's two presidential campaigns, now a presidential advisor, and widely referred to as "Bush's Brain"—gave us a fascinating study of the difference between lying and BS in one sentence. Reported widely was a speech at a fund-raising dinner in New York City in which Rove reported that in the days following the tragedy of September 11, 2001, conservatives "prepared for war" but "liberals," he said, were suggesting "therapy and understanding for our attackers." In reporting that liberals advocated "therapy" for the attackers, Rove was bearing false witness; all nineteen attackers died in the four plane crashes and, therefore, were presumably not available for counseling. His report on who was and was not supporting war also sacrificed truth. The only military intervention being *publicly* discussed in the days following 9/11 related to dismantling the Taliban government in Afghanistan; Democrats in Congress supported *that* about as strongly as Republicans. His charge that liberals were obviously wrong and unpatriotic in wanting to "understand" the attackers was "phony" when viewed from four serious considerations: (1) As the bipartisan congressional investigation concluded, if our leaders had *understood* the Islamic terrorist culture better, we might have prevented 9/11. (2) Anyone who travels knows that many of the earth's peoples (not just Arabic peoples) feel like the world's superpower does not understand them and does not care to; that feeling *might* fuel hostility. (3) Anyone who does not travel can observe that our present government is very concerned that much of the world does not understand us (and continues to assume that a better "public relations" campaign can fix that); there is little interest, however, in "us" understanding "them." (4) Rove appears to be oblivious to the most important principle of strategic warfare—understanding the enemy.

OKAY, LET'S TALK AS CHRISTIANS ABOUT SOME SPECIFIC POLITICAL ISSUES

If evangelical Christians will engage in an honest comparison of the two major parties, there are well-known objectives and causes in a Republican platform that evangelical Christians can and should support. (I will feature three such causes in the next chapter. I support those perspectives, and I often commend and explain them when I am with Democrats.) There are also objectives and causes in a Democratic platform that evangelical Christians can and should support; I have been known to commend and explain these causes in conversations with Republicans. Since many evangelicals are less aware of these causes, let me feature three:

1. People of biblical faith are called to love, preserve, and restore the natural environment upon which we and all other creatures depend. If any Bible-believing reader experiences doubt about our responsibility to creation, I need to ask you one embarrassing

question: What is it about the Lord's mandate in Genesis to be "stewards" of his creation that you don't understand? While scientists seldom reach unanimity on anything, the scientific consensus on global warming, air and water pollution, glacier melting, soil depletion, the extinction of many species, and other serious threats to God's good creation is about as compelling as science ever gets. California (Republican) Governor Arnold Schwarzenegger consulted a range of authorities and declared, "The debate is over. We know the science, we see the threat, and we know the time for action is now."[1] Some other Republicans (apparently including the president), however, are still in denial. Indeed, they can still find a few scientists who are willing to express "doubt" about the case for global warming and a polluted earth.[2] The data, however, warranting a "preemptive strike" to save the environment are enormously more compelling than data used to support the war in Iraq.

When I tried to explain the biblical mandate to care for creation to the Republican state senator who "stimulated" me to write this book, he assured me that *all* of the environmental advocates who had lobbied the Kentucky Legislature were only "tree huggers," who were not worth taking seriously. But Jesus taught us that the plants matter to God, and God grieves when a wounded sparrow falls to the earth. If Jesus is right and the senator is wrong, then some of the "tree huggers" may be on the side of the angels, and creation's exploiters may be God's enemies, even if they have been baptized and tote King James Bibles.

A century ago, the Republican Party of Teddy Roosevelt clearly perceived that nature was even then threatened, and Republicans led the charge for conservation. The "Rough Rider" observed,[3] "Conservation and rural-life policies are really two sides of the same policy, and down at bottom this policy rests upon the fundamental law that neither man nor nation can prosper unless, in dealing with the present, thought is steadily taken for the future." (Anyone can observe Roosevelt's wisdom first hand, I am told, by visiting Haiti—where the forests are gone and the soil is depleted, and poverty is therefore more entrenched than ever.) By the 1950s and 1960s, however, many Republicans had contracted partial amnesia. Adlai Stevenson once declared in a speech in 1952 that "Nixon is the kind of politician who would cut down a redwood tree, then mount the stump for a speech on conservation."

Today, we no longer expect Republicans to even speak on the topic. In the early twentieth century, many of our evangelical predecessors supported Teddy Roosevelt and his party on this issue because they were right. On this issue, the Republican Party is no longer the party of Teddy Roosevelt. For nearly a century, the United States experienced a political consensus on conservation that every president supported from Teddy Roosevelt through Bill Clinton. George H. W. Bush aspired to be "the environmental president," but his son is allowing his people to overturn the consensus and return to the nineteenth-century policy that made government into industry's co-conspirator in the exploitation of the earth for profit. Since the Democratic Party is now more ecologically informed and serious, let's support them on this cause—while calling Republicans out of their amnesia. If we humans fail to protect and to heal the creation that is entrusted to our stewardship, we and many other species are doomed and most other moral and ethical issues are superfluous. (Why not begin with signing, and cooperating with, the Kyoto Treaty?)

2. The biblical revelation has been clear, since the Exodus of the Hebrew people from captivity in Egypt, that God is on the side of oppressed peoples. Furthermore, Jesus launched his public ministry by identifying with Isaiah's vision that captives would be released and "the oppressed go free." The very early Christian movement was a negligible minority in a Roman Empire headed by a monarch, with no leverage on an issue as enormous as slavery; within the range of what was possible, the movement encouraged Christian masters to treat slaves as sisters and brothers in the faith. By the late fourth century, however, the church was large, did have influence, and was en route to becoming the state religion. Saint Patrick, the evangelist to the Irish, however, was the only bishop to speak out against slavery for hundreds

of years. It took many centuries for a critical mass of Christian leaders to be assaulted by a blinding flash of the obvious. In America's mid-nineteenth century, with the leadership of Abraham Lincoln, the Republican Party arose as Providence's avant-garde for the liberation of enslaved and oppressed people; the Democrats, led by Stephen A. Douglas, used excuses that were tired, even then, to resist slavery's abolition. In one of their celebrated 1858 Senate campaign debates, Douglas raised the specter of interracial marriage. Lincoln responded: "Mr. Douglas, I reject that counterfeit argument which assumes that, just because I do not want a [black] woman for a slave, I must necessarily want her for a wife."

Evangelical Christians, such as Charles G. Finney, Theodore Weld, and Harriet Beecher Stowe, catalyzed and populated the nineteenth-century abolitionist movement, and on this issue they cooperated with the Republicans. The historic success of abolition, in time, has brought to the surface successor issues around human freedom, and people of evangelical faith are still called to love and advance the freedom of the nation's peoples, and the earth's peoples—involving a range of causes from civil rights, to human rights, to religious rights. The two parties today are more mixed than in Lincoln's time. The Republicans seem to be clearer about the need for religious rights in nations such as China; we should support them, while influencing more Democrats to support this cause. In regard to civil rights and human rights, the Republican Party can no longer claim the mantle of Lincoln, but the Democrats do support such causes; we should support them, while influencing more Republicans to reclaim what was once their cause.

3. Since we follow the Prince of Peace, world peace should be much more of a cause for evangelicals than most of us have demonstrated in recent history. With the major (tragic) exception of the medieval Crusades, the church has *generally* opposed war, and some traditions (such as Anabaptists, Quakers, Moravians, and Mennonites) have raised their opposition to war to the level of a doctrinal commitment, which they believe is mandated by Scripture. Depending upon our specific theological

roots, our *only* two ethical options regarding war are Christian pacifism and just war. Some evangelical public leaders (such as William Jennings Bryan) once advocated a strong biblically informed pacifism; Bryan regarded his stand against the Republican's manifest destiny-brand of American imperialism as a righteous cause, to which he called other believers. He saw no place for war in the kingdom of God.

Later evangelical political leaders, such as Mark Hatfield and Jimmy Carter, have believed that "just wars" are occasionally necessary. (According to Christian just war theory, not all wars are equally just; indeed, most just war theorists believe that most wars are unjust. So, for instance, a valid military intervention in Afghanistan to defeat the terrorists and their Taliban protectors does not mean that a war initiated in Iraq or Iran or North Korea or Cuba would be equally valid.) The doctrine of holy war has no precedent in serious Christian thought for (at least) the last eight hundred years. The new doctrine of "preemptive war" has no precedent at all, is impossible to build an alliance upon, and (as we have discovered) has enormous potential for folly. (A generation of Republicans, led by presidents like Harding, Coolidge, and Hoover, had such a strong convictional bias against war that they were labeled isolationists. In this area, too, Republicans have departed from their visionary roots.)

Let me suggest a little Christian common sense. War, for informed Christians, is a *last* resort, and cooperation with other nations (even if it is clumsy and takes longer) is vastly preferable to a unilateral go-it-alone policy. One reason that cooperation is preferable is that the global encounter with terrorism will require more human and physical resources than our one nation can deploy. (We might even do the homework necessary to understand *why* militant Muslims feel so threatened by the westernization and secularism that are now globally exported and to discover some of the causes behind their *jihad* that we could do something about. If this suggestion sounds soft, we might recall, with General Patton, that understanding the enemy is the first principle of effective warfare.)

NOTES

1. As quoted in a *New York Times* editorial, "Global Warming's Reality Putting Bush in Hot Seat," reprinted in *The Lexington Herald Leader* (June 16, 2005), A13.

2. Someone mused that these scientists are direct descendants of the scientists who once assured us that cigarettes are not addictive and do not cause cancer.

3. Theodore Roosevelt, "Rural Life," American Problems, vol. 16 of *The Works of Theodore Roosevelt*, national ed., chapter 20 (New York: Scribner, 1926), 146.

CHAPTER EIGHT

ON SUPPORTING BOTH PARTIES ON SOME ISSUES

All political parties change over time, of course, in part because the world changes and the issues change, but the Republican Party has changed remarkably. Republicans once championed the environment, the infrastructure, civil rights, peace, corporate responsibility, and even balanced budgets. Their Brady Bill once advanced the cause of responsible gun control. Today, the more ideological Republicans are quick to brand as "liberal" most of the big ideas that their party once stood for.

The nation, with much of the world, struggles with other issues. One, for instance, is health care. Since our Lord put himself squarely on the side of health and healing, there would be reasons to support the Democrat proposal that we join the many other "developed" nations and make good health care available for *all* of our people. If Canada (and even the French) can do it, we can too, and learning from them, we can do it better. We'd better learn from them. Toyota recently announced plans for a large new automobile plant in Canada. Several states in the USA had bid for the plant, but Toyota chose a site in Canada *because of* that nation's health care system that serves everyone. In the twenty-first century, as more and more companies struggle to fund adequate health care for their people, many multinational companies will prefer to locate their plants in nations with good national health care programs.

The penal system is another issue that comes to mind. Since Jesus and his apostles believed that all sorts of people could be redeemed and restored, we might support the Democrats (and any Republicans) who want our prison system to breed fewer sophisticated criminals and rehabilitate more of this population.

In the present climate, many evangelical Christians now assume that there are *only* about three public issues that warrant serious evangelical concern: homosexual marriage, abortion, and (more recently) Intelligent Design. As a reflective evangelical, I usually find myself in concert with thoughtful Republicans on these three issues, often for reasons additional to theirs.

For instance, I cannot support the idea of "homosexual marriages" because the Christian doctrine of marriage has, for well over one thousand years, avowed and insisted that the *first* purpose of matrimony is the procreation and rearing of children. The *only* arrangement prescribed in the New Testament for fulfilling God's mandate to "be fruitful and multiply" (Gen. 1:28) is a committed monogamous marriage between one woman and one man. (This is no narrow doctrinaire perspective; most human societies, on every inhabited continent, have developed a similar understanding.)[1] Historically, the church has also long recognized that the committed covenantal relationship between a married man and woman is the *second* purpose for marriage. In very recent history (related to the emergence of birth control), millions of Christians have made the second purpose primary, at least for them. In response to that shift, in which the committed relationship is now defined as the essence

72

of marriage, many gay and lesbian dyads have said that they are committed to each other, that their relationship is meaningful too. So they clamor for the right to be married as heterosexual couples are.

Their campaign has had the useful, if unintended, effect of catalyzing some of us in the church to recover our full doctrine of marriage. Furthermore, we need to nuance the facts with as much precision as we can. Some heterosexual married couples have more children than others, and some can have no children at all; their marriage can still be profoundly meaningful. In each generation, the total population of heterosexual couples has managed to perpetuate the human species; it is reasonable to assume that a sufficient number of married couples will continue to be "fruitful." At the same time, human society cannot count on homosexual dyads to fulfill the first purpose of marriage. Within the doctrine of matrimony, calling *any* other dyad a marriage would make no sense. Since the term "civil union" is a euphemism for marriage, the same critique would apply.

However, our society could reflect on whether we want to recognize "domestic partners" who would, say, share property and health and pension benefits, like married couples do. We have, for decades, observed many dyads (such as sisters, hometown friends, or fraternity buddies, or television's *Odd Couple*) who shared a home that either person, alone, could not have managed; they share expenses and experiences, they help and cover for each other, and one feeds the cat when the other travels. Their relationship is not sexual, but they depend on each other, and they enjoy the arrangement. They do not pretend that their friendship is more, or other, than it is. In the "Bush economy," with a net decline of several million jobs that permit a middle-class standard of living, with more and more people whose incomes cannot sustain the lifestyle of their parents, the number of *de facto* domestic partnerships is increasing. A plausible case can be made, say, for shared health benefits, or a mutual inheritance agreement, or pension benefits continuing for one when the other dies. Christians ought to encourage this public discussion. There would be no good reasons, however, to confine domestic partnership recognition, and benefits, to dyads who say their relationship is sexual. *If* we do it, let's extend benefits to any two (or three, or four) people who develop (for whatever reasons) a functioning domestic partnership.

———∞∞——   ———∞∞——   ———∞∞——

While several of the views I have expressed earlier represent more continuity with where the Republican Party *used* to be than where it is today, I also side with many contemporary Republicans on the issue of abortion. One reason is personal: I am a former fetus who believes that other fetuses should have the same inalienable right to life that I would want for myself. The other reason is rooted in the remarkable degree to which evangelical Christianity, Roman Catholic Christianity, and medical science now concur that viable human life begins *much* earlier in a mother's womb than the crowd who regards abortion as merely another method of contraception has ever acknowledged. (*Some* pro-choice advocates *still* try to deny the evidence for early viability, thereby demonstrating that the capacity for denial is broadly, not narrowly, distributed in the whole population.) I have discovered, however, that this crowd is smaller than we evangelicals assume, and the common ground is more extensive than we assume.

For instance, many (I think most) pro-choice Democrats are *not* "for" abortion. They do not want more abortions; they want fewer abortions, and they would celebrate if there were none. They agree that unwanted pregnancies should not occur, but they do. When they do, they believe (with Republicans like Barbara Bush) that the decision should finally rest with the mother. Some people do not want to return to the days when abortion was outlawed—a period in which many desperate women felt driven to back-alley operations by barbaric surgeons. They believe that our society must provide other options (such as interim support, health insurance, day care, and adoption) for women who have experienced an unwanted pregnancy.

I am suggesting that those of us who want a world with *no* abortions may be called to work with, and influence, the *many* people who want *fewer* abortions, and this is an opportunity in which Christians who have some capital with Republicans should spend it. For example, there was a period in President Clinton's second term in which he was willing to cooperate with a Republican majority in Congress on the issue of abortion. Many children would now be alive if politicians had accepted some compromises.[2]

May I also suggest that pro-life evangelical Christians have an opportunity to be more consistently pro-life than much of our society now perceives us to be? If we really believe, as we often say, that abortion is wrong because the affirmation of life "trumps" all other values, then (logically) we would join the people who work (say) for serious gun control and a healthy creation, and we would oppose war and capital punishment, without apologizing for moral consistency (or rationalizing our way out of it).

―――⟊――――――――⟊――――――――⟊―――

Three generations after the Scopes Trial, creation and evolution are in the news[3] and on school board agendas once again, plus a newer term—*Intelligent Design.* People on one side want Intelligent Design taught in the nation's science classrooms (often in addition to evolution—which, they contend, should be presented only as a theory). People on the other side oppose the teaching of Intelligent Design in science classrooms because, they say, evolution is science and Intelligent Design is not science, but only warmed-over creationism. Furthermore, they add, creationism posits the existence of God—a topic that is not within the province of science; and, because God is assumed, teaching Intelligent Design would violate the First Amendment principle of the separation of church and state. Several observations are germane to the politics of this discussion:

First, while Intelligent Design advocates typically believe in a God who created the cosmos, their approach is much more consistent with the church's perennial interest (for most of twenty centuries) in God's natural revelation than with early twentieth-century creationism—which advocated that schools should teach creation because the Bible teaches it. Intelligent Design is especially rooted in the early nineteenth-century philosophy of William Paley. Paley, in 1800, proposed his now-famous watchmaker analogy in *Natural Theology*: If, while hiking, one discovered a large rock, partly buried in the earth beside the path, one might reasonably assume that the rock got there for no particular reason, has always been there, and has always been much like one found it. However, if you found a watch beside the path, you would not assume it has always been there, nor that it has always been like this. Because you are familiar with a watch's purpose, you know that some creative intelligence designed it and made it—for the purpose of telling time. Paley believed that we could likewise infer a Designer behind some of the complex objects of nature that serve significant purposes, such as the human eye. Indeed, he even believed that we could infer from nature the existence of a wise and benevolent God.

Charles Darwin once admired Paley's philosophy, but following the cruel and protracted death of his nine-year-old daughter, he became acutely aware of imperfection and injustice in nature. In time, as he reflected upon his observations of animal species in different natural settings, he concluded that species survive (and evolve) through adaptation to their environment and that, apparently, this "natural selection" occurs randomly, with no transcendent purpose behind it. For a century, Darwin's theory of evolution seemed to trump, and eclipse, Paley's line of thought. In the 1980s, however, new discoveries in biology convinced a growing number of scholars that Darwin's theory could not sufficiently account for the remarkable complexity of some objects in nature that serve an apparent purpose—such as the human eye.

While the evolution school of thought has a longer history than the Intelligent Design school, it is becoming more and more difficult to say that the first represents science and the second does not. Neither conducts scientific experiments per se; both rely on inference from observation. Scientists with Ph.D.'s in fields ranging from zoology, genetics, and chemistry to philosophy, mathematics, and astrophysics, populate both camps. The two schools often study the same objects (like cells and molecules and fossil evidence); they often derive insight from the same data (or the same studies); some scholars infer Purpose from the data and discern the fingerprints of God, and some do not. This division in human perception is *very* longstanding; we see it reflected in the four Gospels. When Jesus healed sick, lame, or possessed people, some bystanders perceived that God was acting through Jesus' ministry, but some did not; some even concluded that the evil one was in him, while others were upset that he had violated a Jewish Sabbath custom by working on the seventh day of the week. So the data in science and religion can function something like the inkblots in Rorschach tests; what one perceives says as much about the perceiver as about the data.

In my field of evangelization, this may be the most profound issue we struggle with (and *never* fully resolve): *Why* do some people believe, and some do not? Some people, as in Charles Darwin's case, come to profound doubt through a disappointing or painful experience. Some people, as in a dozen or more Libertarians I have interviewed, want to live their lives without constraints or rules; they often become atheists, agnostics, or deists, which means, in any of these variations, that there is no God to whom they are accountable. With some people, God does not fit their expectation of what God should be like, or what God should do. (First-century Jewish people, for instance, expected that God's Messiah would come as a Davidic military king, who would defeat the Romans and restore Israel to greatness; when Jesus came, instead, in the model of Isaiah's "Suffering Servant," the people missed the day of their visitation. Some people were not raised in a family of faith, or their peers are not people of faith, or they are inculturated in an ideology (like Marxism or secularism) that leaves little room for faith, so they are less likely to believe. We have always known that some people love their sins too much to give them up and live for God. Some people do not live in a social network that includes credible inviting Christians, so they have never had a valid opportunity to become people of faith. I could add reasons from other types of cases, but some people apparently lack faith for reasons we do not understand. (John Calvin's classic conclusion that some people are not of the "elect," i.e., apparently they were not created with the capacity for faith, is one way to resolve this dilemma.)

—∞∞—   —∞∞—   —∞∞—

At least four comments are warranted from this discussion. First, we can be thankful that Darwin reminds us of our kinship with other creatures; the Bible has always taught this, but many of us did not "get it" from our primary source. Second, even if one is able to infer from creation a Creative Intelligence operative behind the natural world, this only leads to deism—which is a long way from the Christian understanding of Saving Faith; any reading of a "General Revelation" still needs to be completed by the gospel's "Special Revelation." Third, Christians have no monopoly on intolerant dogmatism. When evolution's most aggressive advocates insist on deciding in advance what conclusions we are *not* free to reach and teach from scientific data, we should call that game by its right name and encourage them (at least) toward greater scientific objectivity and openness. Fourth, this whole discussion illustrates how, often, knowledge no longer fits in the categories of our academic disciplines. It may be that neither Intelligent Design nor evolution fully fits the science paradigm. Darwin's *Origin of Species* is part science and part (naturalistic) philosophy. It was Darwin's philosophy of evolution that seemed to support the European Enlightenment's doctrine of inevitable progress. Likewise, capitalists were standing on Darwin's shoulders when they developed social Darwinism—contending that people compete for survival, wealth, and status and that "superior" people and social groups become powerful and wealthy. Again, Darwin's paradigm was indispensable in the Marxist development of the philosophy of dialectical materialism to explain the growth and development of human history.

President Bush recently suggested that both perspectives, evolution and Intelligent Design, should be taught in schools. "Part of education," he observed, "is to expose people to different schools of thought."[4] This, of course, is *supposed* to be public education's policy. Let's support the policy's restoration and trust that local schools and school boards are competent to adjust the curriculum to fit emerging knowledge.

A response to the charge that to teach Intelligent Design would violate the Constitution will be apparent in the discussion of the First Amendment in the next chapter.

If I support an informed Republican perspective on abortion, gay marriage, and Intelligent Design, the reader would reasonably expect me to be a card-carrying Republican. I cannot say that I have never considered it. But I am still an evangelical Christian "Republocrat" with Democratic sympathies, because the Republican Party has abandoned many principles once dear to evangelicals, because Democrats need more evangelical Christians working with them, and also because I remain grateful for the remarkable humane achievements of the Democratic Party in the twentieth century. (I am not referring, however, to the excesses of the sixties nor to the "politically correct" agenda that recently drove one wing of Democrats, though that fervor has cooled.) Consider the following litany of Democratic achievements.

- The Democrats, under FDR's "New Deal," catalyzed America's recovery from the Great Depression in which millions of people lost their farms, homes, or jobs. When Roosevelt was elected, unemployment exceeded 25 percent. New laws strengthened banks, farms, industries, and laboring people. The government employed people on a larger scale, and they built schools, highways, roads, bridges, dams, parks, and other public works. I received my early education in two of those schools and I played baseball in one of those parks—and the era's roads got me to these places.

- In my part of the country, the Tennessee Valley Authority provided affordable electricity for the first time to millions of people in a vast region. As I write this, my Mac is powered by the electricity made possible in FDR's era.
- FDR launched the Social Security program, which provided insurance for unemployed people and pensions for retired people. From my dad's inheritance plus his Social Security benefits, my deaf mother lived her last fifteen years with dignity and without feeling like a burden to her son.
- Medicare, another Democrat creation, has transformed old age in the United States; the society decided to stop abandoning people who can no longer work and declared that they are still of great value to the nation. My mother never had to do without the medicine her physician prescribed. She experienced several catastrophic illnesses in her last years; Medicare, combined with supplemental health insurance, protected her from financial devastation.
- The Democrats, working incrementally through several presidents and congresses, liberated our land from its version of apartheid and guaranteed civil rights for African Americans and all other people. I was raised in the South that still experienced segregated schools, restaurants, lunch counters, and restrooms. I do not miss that obscenity, and I stand politically opposed to the people who do seem to miss it.
- While Democrats never got the Equal Rights Amendment ratified, they advanced the rights and status of women by several light years. We now see women in many roles, like corporate executives, news anchors, and university presidents, which were closed to women before. The Democrats' Title IX legislation opened much fuller participation to women in sports. To my knowledge, it has never

occurred to my Republican friend who cheers for his daughter, the power forward on the local high school girl's basketball team, that he can thank the other party for the growth of women's sports that she and he enjoy.

This litany of gratitude could be extended. If you enjoy clear air or clean water, you have some Democrats to thank. If you have a family member with a mental illness who is less stigmatized, more understood, and better served than a generation ago, you have some Democrats to thank. Democrats have believed in the government's mandate, from the Constitution, "to promote the general welfare." They inspired three generations of idealistic people to devote their lives to public service, including the Peace Corps. They gave the country a school lunch program, and Head Start, and food stamps. They advanced police protection in most of our communities, they integrated the armed forces, and they gave our troops the GI Bill. I remain astonished at how many people took advantage of much of this, and more, who in time prospered and became middle class and then forgot where they came from and how they got there. Like Clarence Thomas, they started believing the myth of "individualistic self-reliance." They now view themselves as "self-made"; they did it all themselves. May I suggest that on this issue Hillary Clinton is right? "It takes a village to raise a child." None of us made it on our own. God, and some people, and a society, believed in us and invested in us and provided many of the links in the chain that we, at the time, could not have provided. Our ancestors now call us to pass it on.

I once had a visit with Claude Pepper, at one time a senator from Florida, later the longtime congressman from Miami, and a legendary New Deal Democrat. In time, he became the oldest serving congressman. He sponsored much of the legislation that now supports senior citizens. He always spoke with moral fervor and often in hyperbole. I asked him "What drives your career in public service?" He said that some people are born with the deck stacked against them, and sooner or later, almost everyone else gets sick, or down on their luck, or needs help beyond their means, so they need a society that believes in them and supports them enough to see them through. "When the Republicans see someone struggling," he said, "they advise them to go inherit an oil well." He continued, the "Republican solution" is not an option for most people, so they need "a government that practices the Golden Rule."

NOTES

1. Some societies once practiced polygyny, but "advanced" into monogamy. Most (if not all) of the societies that still practice polygyny also prioritize the procreation and rearing of children; homosexual marriages cannot perpetuate the species.

2. A number of studies demonstrate correlations like the following. When the unemployment (and underemployment) rates are high, more men do not marry. When a woman experiences an unplanned pregnancy, if she has no husband, and/or believes she cannot afford to raise the baby, and/or lacks health insurance, she is more likely to choose abortion. Such correlations argue, if we really are "pro-life," for universal health insurance and economic policies that encourage the creation of good jobs.

3. See the *Time* cover story "The Evolution Wars" (August 15, 2005, vol. 166, number 7), 26ff.

4. Roundtable interview of President Bush by reporters from Texas newspapers on August 1, 2005.

EVANGELICAL CHRISTIANITY'S UNIQUE OPPORTUNITIES TO CONTRIBUTE TO AMERICAN POLITICAL LIFE

In several issues of great importance, if evangelical Christians do not make their contribution, no one else is likely to; indeed, many people may not even acknowledge the issues' existence. Take, for instance, the twin conspiracy of silence that entrenches the United States in two complex issues: church and state, and gun control. Over virtually no one's constitutional protest, politics has expanded two themes in the Bill of Rights far beyond what the Constitution's framers had in mind, and the issues and problems have become so convoluted that a return to the original meaning of the Constitution's framers is the only resolution. I am proposing that we demonstrate that we are "strict constructionists" by "strictly construing" the first two amendments in the Bill of Rights.

Let's be specific. The First Amendment to the Constitution provides that "Congress shall make no law respecting an establishment of religion, or prohibiting the free exercise thereof."[1] When you read the founders' deliberations, the amendment meant only one thing: The United States would *not* have a "state church" like most European nations had then, and many have today. There would be no "official" or "established" church that, like the (Anglican) Church of England, or the (Lutheran) National Church of Denmark, or the Russian Orthodox Church, might marginalize (or even oppress) other churches and their people. The young country was committed to religious freedom; indeed, no laws would be permitted "prohibiting the free exercise" of religion. Advocates and movements for the separation of church and state, including many left of center, have been permitted to stretch the meaning of the First Amendment far beyond anything the Constitution's framers had in mind. D. James Kennedy is right; the framers never intended that Christianity must be absent from the nation's life or that Christianity must have no influence in our government's priorities and policies. The intention of the Constitution was to include (not to exclude) Christianity in the nation's life, but to give no church or denomination a privileged place or role in the nation's life.[2] (This has many applications; for instance, making the Intelligent Design perspective available in a school's curriculum would not thereby grant "establishment" to any one church.) That is all it meant; virtually everything else that history has attached to it is accretion. Conservatives have not consistently challenged the First Amendment's distortion, however, because many of them (such as hunters and other gun enthusiasts) have had an interest in swelling the *Second* Amendment beyond what any founders would recognize.

The Second Amendment to the Constitution declared, "A well regulated militia, being necessary to the security of a free state, the right of the people to keep and bear arms shall not be infringed." That amendment, too, has a very specific referent. It meant *only* that any and all states in the union might have an armed militia if they choose, and the federal government may not contravene that right. (Conditions have changed, of course, so we may ask whether, say, Delaware *still* needs a state militia for its security. Nevertheless, the state still has the constitutional right to bear arms.) The Second Amendment stands, objectively read, as an explicit expression of states' rights. In the last half century, however, fueled by the lavish funds and lobbying efforts of the National Rifle Association, firearms manufacturers, distributors, and merchants have wrapped the Second Amendment around their commercial interests. They have extended the amendment's meaning to block any attempt by government to control the sale and ownership of firearms. Decades ago, they began their campaign by advocating the right of hunters to own shotguns, but the later accretions added to the Second Amendment are even more grotesque than those attached to the First.

In the Second Amendment, the Constitution's framers were *only* focusing on the rights of any state to have its own militia. The founders never, even once, considered the ludicrous idea that your crazy neighbor down the street has an inalienable right to own assault weapons. The NRA-sponsored accretions to the Second Amendment have contributed to a murder rate in the United States that far exceeds that of other "civilized" countries. They have seduced millions of people with the slogan "Guns don't kill people, people kill people." The slogan, of course, ignores the fact that when people kill people, they usually kill them *with* something other than their bare hands—something more likely to kill the person, with a lesser risk to the killer, like (say) a gun. The slogan's fallacy is revealed in the fact that no one even considers any parallel expressions. In the buildup to the war in Iraq, for instance, *no one* suggested that "Weapons of mass destruction don't kill people, people kill people."

For too long, supporters of an incredible expansion of the First Amendment's meaning have kept quiet about the Second Amendment's expansion, and vice versa. It is a long, remarkable, if unacknowledged, conspiracy of silence. (By mutual agreement, no one will "strictly construe" either of the first two amendments.) If serious public Christians do not expose the twin fraud for what it is, who else will? Besides, Christians have a stake in being publicly faithful to the original meanings of the first two amendments, and we have reasons to oppose the parasitic barnacles that history has attached to them.

While the Bill of Rights provides two of the great opportunities for Christian involvement to make a difference in this land, our changing world has provided a third. Peter Drucker, the guru of the twentieth-century revolution in management, died at age 95 in November 2005. Most of the tributes ignored his most significant book, *The Age of Discontinuity*, which featured his most significant insight: We no longer live in a world in which the two traditional categories, "personal" and "social," are adequate to frame our understanding of the world. In between those two categories, a third has emerged: "The large organization is the environment of man in modern society."[3] Furthermore, the world of organizations and institutions in which most of us study and earn our living and pursue other interests has become much larger, more specialized, and more permanent than anyone projected even a century ago. In his later writing, Peter Drucker demonstrated that, in a complex world of large specialized organizations, each organization develops its own "culture" *and* is increasingly dependent upon many other organizations. Drucker devoted his prodigious career to discovering how to lead and manage effective organizations and how to orchestrate an effective society of organizations.

Peter Drucker perceived early that an adequate ethic must drive an organization—to ensure integrity in its contribution to society and in its treatment of the organization's people. Drucker's ethical vision for organizations has often been compromised. When thoughtful Christians have realized that they live in a democratic society but work for a totalitarian company, or when they have observed company presidents receiving bonuses while jeopardizing the people's pension fund, or when they observe companies knowingly marketing unreliable or unsafe products, they know this should not be. Christians with an ethical kingdom vision are called to see a changed world, a world of organizations, that stands in serious need of Christianity's prophetic witness. We want the will of God to be done in our organizations, as well as in our personal lives, and on earth, as in heaven. The world of organizations may become the greatest theater of significant Christian reform in this century. If Christians do not sound this trumpet and lead the way, however, no one else is likely to.

By being involved in both parties, evangelical Christians also have the opportunity to help restore the two major political parties to something like the greater health they once displayed and the greater contribution they once made. In 2000, Ralph Nader justified his third party campaign for the presidency by claiming that the two major parties were just alike, were controlled by the same special interests, and stood for the same things, so voters had no real choice. The early history of the twenty-first century has demonstrated that Nader could not have been more wrong. For one thing, the two parties are somewhat controlled by *different* special interests. For another, they were healthier and contributed more when they *did* see the world in more similar ways, and did largely agree on the issues and on the objectives for which the country should live, even if they disagreed on the priorities within the objectives or the best ways to achieve them.

Once upon a time, in other words, the two parties actually reflected upon and discussed all of the issues within each party. The reason was because there were many thinking people in the Democratic Party who were in the center, or even right of center, on many issues; there were many thinking people in the Republican Party who were in the center, or even left of center, on many issues. They often talked to each other, and even heard and understood each other, and stimulated each other's best thought—within each respective party. The Democratic Party had more states' rights people and pro-life people than now; the Republican Party had more environmentalists and penal reform advocates than now. (The list goes on.) Party platforms were serious documents that represented something like the full range of wisdom available within each party; their planks read more like nuanced positions, and less like slogans, than today. I can remember when some voters actually *read* the platforms of both parties, because they were reasoned, and worth reading, and the presidential candidates actually ran on, rather than away from, the party platform.

It turns out that when the two parties had broader views within their ranks, the political party system (which is nowhere provided for in the Constitution) added a nearly indispensable component to the system of "checks and balances" that the Constitution's framers otherwise provided for. Every issue, and every significant perspective upon it, was first deliberated within each party. People of the winning position had heard, and often understood, other points of view; the final proposal often represented some "compromise" with the contrasting wisdom within the party; and the people knew that "compromise" is *not* synonymous with "surrender." The position that pooled the most intelligence was usually much better than any one ideological group would have arrived at by itself.

In more recent years, as the parties have become more ideologically homogeneous, almost every proposal they offer the nation is the product of less deliberation and more social influence. Since their idea received no serious challenge while it was developing within the party, its advocates are now inclined to see it as obvious Truth. The stage is thereby fully set for Groupthink, which has never served this nation well. Groupthink has much less chance of hijacking a party's thinking, however, when its deliberations are really open to a wide range of ideas. Christians who are present in both parties could find ways to insist on healthy process.

Christians could also find ways to insist on more competent candidates for public leadership. The partisan spirit of our time has been more passionate about finding someone who can win an election than about finding someone who can govern if elected. The 2004 presidential campaign serves as a pristine example. Press releases in May 2005 revealed that John Kerry graduated from Yale with a grade point average of 76; Bush graduated two years later with an average of 77. (Yale's grading system at the time pegged a numerical grade between 70 and 79 as a "C.") While "book learning" is not everything, none of us would knowingly choose a surgeon, or a tax accountant, or an airline pilot who had taken his or her education as casually as Bush and Kerry seemingly took theirs. *Competence*, of course, is not the same as education and it matters more than education per se; in our astonishingly complex world, however, world-class competence is not possible without an education that is both broad and deep.[4] As Harry Truman once taught us, "Not all readers are leaders, but all great leaders are readers."

The need for knowledge-based competence is not restricted to the presidency; it is imperative for the leaders of the government's many agencies. The nation perceived this, with astonishing clarity, in the events following the decimation of the Gulf Coast by Hurricane Katrina in September 2005. For days, the Federal Emergency Management Agency (FEMA) was incapable of orchestrating much response to challenges like rescuing stranded people, deploying food, water, and other life essentials, and restoring basic services to New Orleans. Investigations then revealed that FEMA's director, Michael Brown, was a political patronage appointment with little experience in disaster management. Later investigations revealed that FEMA had responded incompetently to many lesser disasters in recent years. The South Florida Sun-Sentinel "examined 20 of the 313 disasters declared by FEMA from 1999 through 2004 . . . Of the $1.2 billion FEMA paid in those disasters, 27 percent went to areas where official reports showed only minor damage or none at all."[5] One official explained that FEMA is now "folded" into the Department of Homeland Security—which, following 9/11, is now more focused on terrorism than natural disasters; but if terrorists had bombed the levees near New Orleans and flooded the city, would the response have been any more capable? There is no reason to believe that FEMA is the only agency that has lacked sufficiently resolute and competent leadership. There are reasons to believe that the Environmental Protection Agency, the Food and Drug Administration, the Treasury Department, the Defense Department, and others are afflicted with FEMA Syndrome.

In the post-Katrina political climate, more Americans are now aware (at least for the time being) that competence matters. In that climate, President Bush nominated his devoted personal attorney, Harriet Miers, to succeed Sandra Day O'Connor as an associate justice on the Supreme Court. An astonishing range of leaders and organizations (particularly conservatives) observed that the nominee had neither a record of constitutional scholarship, nor judicial experience, nor other attributes that strongly commended her for that role. So many people in the president's base said "no way" that Miers withdrew her nomination. We must hope that the lesson sticks long enough for us to return to the idea that the most informed and competent people ought to lead in statecraft.

In addition to the remarkable shift that made winning more important then governing, the political climate of our time has deterred many of the most capable (and ethical) people from making themselves available. Why? Many of them do not believe in the "pit bull attack politics" now afflicting American campaigns. They do not want to practice it, or tacitly agree to allow their committees or surrogates to practice it, or to be the objects of that savagery. Most people did something in their past that they would change now if they could, or a skeleton inhabits their closet or an ancestor's closet; they are reluctant to put their families through the pain of exposure, name calling, and the other games of trash politics.[6] We Americans like to think of the United States as a model democracy that other nations would eagerly copy if they understood it. When they visit our land during campaigns, however, they are astonished to see how the parties treat each other; their lack of admiration is transparent.

Christians who believe in redemption could do some things about redeeming the American political system. We can be present and active in both parties as salt and light; we can advocate what we believe to be Christianity's causes in both parties, while identifying with people who want a better world and making friends for Christ; we can remind partisans that "truth" and "justice" are more faithful (and useful) categories for appraising proposals and policies than "conservative" and "liberal." We can encourage committed, competent people to enter, and advance in, public service. Within the party we are involved in, we can challenge trash politics every time it surfaces, while modeling a better way. We can connect with people in the other party who want a healthier public life in this land. We can model what it looks like to *understand* the other party's view, rather than submitting it to immediate distortion. We can help the parties to work publicly (in Lincoln's words) "with malice toward none, with charity for all." We can treat each other, and even "enemies," as brothers and sisters.

This is being written in the year of the two-hundreth anniversary of history's greatest naval battle. In the (1805) Battle of Trafalgar, Admiral Nelson's British fleet of twenty-seven ships met Napoleon's alliance of thirty-three French and Spanish ships off the coast of Portsmouth, England. Such battles typically lasted for several days, but because of Nelson's unprecedented strategy for the battle (later to be called "the Nelson Touch"), the British won in three hours—losing no ships while immobilizing or destroying twenty-two of the thirty-three Franco-Spanish ships, although a musket ball struck Nelson's back, and he died. A journalist reports what happened next. As the French and Spanish were surrendering, "a fierce storm broke out at sea . . . But rather than head for shore, the victorious Britons performed extraordinary feats of seamanship and bravery, saving the lives of thousands of their wounded and exhausted opponents."[7]

Even in warfare, troops sometimes remember that their enemies are (first) their brothers. Would it be possible for party members, in the heat of campaigns, to remember that too? Would that contribute to the kind of nation, and world, that almost everyone really wants? Would this be a worthy life-investment for the people called to be salt and light?

NOTES

1. The amendment continues to guarantee freedom of speech, press, and assembly.

2. Some would point out that the United States' populations now represent many more religions (from astrology to Zen) than the Constitution's framers would have experienced in the 1780s or anticipated for the country's future, so they believe that *Christianity* should now have no visible role in the nation's life unless all religions do. Anyone is free to attempt a reasonable case for that, but not from the First Amendment and the founders' intentions.

3. See Peter F. Drucker, *The Age of Discontinuity: Guidelines to Our Changing Society* (New York: Harper & Row, 1968), 186. Drucker dramatized the emerging world of large organizations with many examples. He reports, for instance, that "big business" had already arrived by the early twentieth century. He notes, however, "'the big business' of 1910 would strike us today as a veritable minnow. The 'octopus' that gave our grandparents nightmares, John D. Rockefeller's Standard Oil Trust, was cut into fourteen pieces by the Supreme Court in 1911. Less than thirty years later, every one of these successor companies was larger than Rockefeller's Standard Oil Trust had been" (173). He demonstrated the trend toward large organizations in many sectors. For instance, "No university in the Western world had more than 5,000 students before 1914" (173). Today, many private universities are at least twice that size; many public universities are at least five times that size, some are ten or twelve times that size. Drucker lived long enough to observe this trend continue in ways he had not predicted—including the rise of major shopping malls, and the rise of "megachurches"—which, he believed, can serve many people through their range of congregations and specialized ministries that smaller traditional churches cannot serve.

4. There is no reason to believe that Kerry and Bush were the most competent people available. Arguably, Kerry is only the second most competent senator from his state, and Bush is only the third most competent person in his family.

5. Sally Kestin, Megan O'Matz, John Maines, and John Burstein, "Newspaper's inquiry finds long history of FEMA fraud," in *The Lexington Herald-Leader* (September 18, 2005), A4.

6. Consider one specific, but recurring example. In the last five presidential elections, Republican leaders and/or their surrogates have attacked the wives of the Democratic candidate. Such "low-blow" campaigning may not always be effective, but understandably, some men are reluctant to submit their wives to public abuse.

7. Thomas Wagner, "Britons, others mark Nelson's 1805 victory," *The Lexington Herald-Leader* (June 29, 2005), A3.

CHAPTER TEN

AN EVANGELICAL "PLATFORM" FOR REACHING DEMOCRATS (AND REPUBLICANS)

O ne purpose of this book is to encourage many evangelical Christians to love, and serve with, Democrats once again. Furthermore, because evangelical Christians have largely abandoned the Democratic Party and its people for a quarter century (and, consequently, fewer of them are now Christian believers), another purpose is to encourage evangelicals to make the life of Christian discipleship a live option for this population once again. I have placed this chapter near the end, lest some Democrats feel patronized by the idea that they, particularly, need to be evangelized. Many Republicans need evangelizing too.

The late Bishop Stephen Neill, the Anglican missionary statesman and scholar, used to observe that people really need to experience "three conversions" if they can become the people that the Christian movement needs and that God meant them to be. People need to turn (1) to Christ, (2) to the Body of Christ—

the church, and (3) to Christ's vision for a restored, just, peaceful, and redeemed world. In Neill's extensive experience, he observed that these three conversions usually take place *one at a time* in a person's life, and they occur *in any conceivable sequence*. He added that many of the people who are a problem to Christianity (and to themselves), who have never experienced abundant life or advanced the church's mission, are people who have experienced one (or two) of the conversions, but not (yet) all three. Christ still invites them, and so must we.

Neill's paradigm helps us perceive the direction of our outreach to many Democrats—and to many Republicans. As a rough generalization, many Democrats have experienced some version of Neill's third conversion—they yearn for a better world, but they have not experienced the first—which mediates grace, reconciliation, second birth and new life. By contrast, many Republicans are confessing Christians who have experienced some version of the first conversion, but they are more interested in going to heaven than in heaven's will being done on earth.

Many Republicans *and* Democrats need the second conversion more than they know because, as John Wesley commented, "Christianity is not a solitary religion." In our time, however, people right of center have often regarded the church as (say) "optional," while people left of center have often regarded it as (say) "obsolete." So, for contrasting reasons, a great many Republicans and Democrats need the church's Scripture, sacraments, support, and spiritual formation as much as any football players have ever needed a coach, a game plan, and the power of the huddle, the crowd, and the half-time pep talk to renew them for the line of scrimmage.

Reality is never as simple as it should be. The church would be wise to give up its prevailing assumption that people who have experienced only the first conversion are Christians, and people who have experienced only the second conversion *might* be, but people who have experienced only the third conversion are not. Everyone needs to experience all three conversions to become the Christian that God wants and the world needs.

Many Republicans and Democrats have experienced some measure of the second conversion only; they are church members, they benefit from the church's ministries, and they may even be regular church attendees; they go through the motions, and think of themselves as Christians, but they have never experienced the adventurous life of the kingdom. I have interviewed many such people; Republicans are more likely nominal Protestants, Democrats are more likely nominal Catholics. They stand in need of the first and third conversions (in either order), but their lengthy exposure to some diluted form of Christianity has immunized them against the full dose. That is why it takes a different approach, or even a different kind of congregation, to engage them with power.

Although the ranks of pre-Christian Democrats have grown in the last generation, Republicans have their fair share of unreached pagans, of (at least) four fairly distinct types.

- For instance, the Republican Party in the United States has some of the people who are more typical of conservative parties in Europe—privately educated, hereditary privileged, upper-upper class, often atheists. Their highest power is Adam Smith's "invisible hand"—a transcendent force that (supposedly) produces the healthiest society when each person is free from restraints to pursue his or her own economic self-interest.
- By comparison, the "Bourbon Republicans" are the newer rich, in fact or in aspiration, who appear to live as isolated as possible from the poor and struggling populations of their city. They may live in gated communities and ride in chauffeured stretch-limos that whisk them to the country club or to the luxury suites at the college football game. The Bourbons, like the hereditary rich, live as materialists but are more likely to be nominal Christians.[1]
- Again, many of the conservative movements (and their people) that support (and also influence) the

Republican Party do not even claim to be Christian. The John Birch Society, for instance, will only say that it professes religious ideals which upon examination are not close to the ethical vision of biblical Christianity. The Libertarian Party, whose people want a free life without constraints, has more than its fair share of atheists, agnostics, and deists. The right-wing white supremacist, anti-Catholic, and vigilante groups, who can be counted on to support Republican candidates, often mistake their ideology for Christianity, but they are now among the *target populations* for Christian mission today.

• Furthermore, the Republicans have the support of most of the white, redneck, "flat earth," anti-intellectual Americans. The party may campaign on one or two themes dear to this population, but their influence upon the party is negligible. This extensive population typically mistakes American civil religion for Christianity and their culture's folk wisdom for the Christian way; I still hear them saying that "People get what they deserve," and "People need to get a life," and "The Lord helps them who helps themselves," and "You've got to know when to hold 'em and know when to fold 'em." They usually want to "do right," and they usually make good neighbors, but their brand of patriotism is often undiluted idolatry.

That list is not exhaustive, but it demonstrates the multiple mission fields in the Republican constituency. Remarkably, however, evangelical Christian Republicans do not seem to evangelize other Republicans; they are so honored to be included at the table, they comply with the moves that make the party's agenda the only priority.

To sum up, we are ambassadors for Christ's church with the people of both political parties. This means that we should point many Republicans toward the third conversion, and many Democrats toward the first. Since the latter have been ignored for so long, reaching Democrats is the focus of the following remarks, but much of what follows is adaptable to reaching almost any population in the West.

What would it look like for more evangelical Christians to join forces with Democrats, while also wanting to be used by God to help pre-Christian Democrats discover something more? One qualifier cries out to be stated now: if, upon reexamination, you are still convinced that the Republican Party and agenda have a near-monopoly on God's purposes in this world, do not even consider "infiltrating" the Democratic Party just to save souls. You would, at least at times, be living in deception. But if you believe that the Lord is not without witness among them, and that some truth and noble purposes might be found among them, then consider becoming a living oxymoron—an "evangelical Democrat" involved in mission with (and to) Democrats. Actually, if your conversation style is not experienced as pushy, manipulative, or obsessive, Democrats will not experience an occasional conversation about Christianity's message and perspective, or (say) an invitation to visit your Sunday school class Christmas party, as intrusive or alien. Their ranks (like Republican ranks) will usually have some people involved who do what they can to influence party members toward their special interest. Spend the most time with the most receptive people, while loving, praying for, and planting seeds in the other people's lives.

If one reason that many of us are called to become involved with the Democratic Party is to make becoming a Christian a live option for more of its people, it might be desirable to reflect momentarily on the *kind* of Christian we believe God has in mind. As I suggested above, many churches in the Judaizing tradition think of Christians as people who believe like us, behave like us, ballot like us, and become like us—culturally, with many churches also expecting that they will be baptized like us and/or have the kind of spiritual experience or religious affections we consider normative. In *Church for the Unchurched,* while affirming the usefulness of many such expectations, I suggest that they are not sufficiently biblical for understanding the essence of being a Christian, and I offer a paradigm that, I believe, is closer to the Christianity of the Apostles and their churches.[2] A Christian is a person who (1) lives in new relationships, (2) lives a new life, and (3) lives out a new lifestyle.

We are, first, talking about the kind of "Christians" who live in two new relationships—a new relationship (or covenant) *with* God—which is informed by the gospel, made possible by God's grace and our faith-response, and is nurtured by prayer; and a new relationship *with the people of God*—the church—which is experienced in the whole body and in its redemptive cells. People generally experience those two new relationships one at a time, and they can occur in either order. Most evangelicals assume the sequence above—that people first experience faith and then they join the fellowship. For most people, however, our own children and outsiders, the sequence is much more often 2-1. Most people belong before they believe, the faith is even more caught than taught.

Those two relationships enable Christians to live a new life— a life that has three indispensable features: (1) Christ's true disciples are called, and committed, to doing *the will of God.* We live no longer for ourselves, or for any selfish agenda, but for God's will for our lives and God's will for the world; (2) Christ's disciples are called to a *life of good will*—primarily for other people, and also for other creatures and for God's whole creation. The Christian's love for people extends to people beyond one's own family, social network, class, nationality, culture and race; and (3) As Christ's disciples, we can experience *freedom* in Christ—from sin, guilt, legalism, memories, dysfunctional feelings and "games," idolatry, peer conformity, obsessions, addictions, evil powers, and anything else that would destroy us, including death.

The new life in Christ deploys us in a new lifestyle, with four distinctive features: (1) Followers of Christ *live in the world, but not of it*; they are driven by kingdom values and not by ideology, or fashion, or the values of Hollywood or Madison Avenue;

(2) We live no longer for ourselves; we now live for Jesus Christ by living for others—through *service and ministry and seeking justice*, doing all the good we can; (3) We follow Christ in *witness and mission*—reaching out to other people we know or can befriend, reaching out to other peoples through mission support, or by going ourselves; and (4) As we follow Jesus Christ, he reveals our true *identity* and gives us the Grace to become the people we were born to be and deeply within us have always yearned to be.

When we reflect upon the essence of being a Christian as new relationships, a new life, and a new lifestyle, to many Christians this does not come as news. This profile features and organizes much of what we already knew but had not known to make central. It does come as news, even good news, to many pre-Christian people. Deep down, many (if not most) secular people really want what Christianity is supposed to be offering. They would love to be reconciled to God and discover their life's purpose, their identity, and so on. One often neglected piece of the ministry of evangelism is helping people to see the target for which God has aimed their lives, to which they are called.

—•—   —•—   —•—

What else is involved in Christian evangelism? One thing that is *not* (or should not) be involved is any kind of manipulation or coercion. Christ wants people's free response to his invitation to "follow me." Another thing that is not (or should not) be involved is a canned presentation of the gospel; what evangelicals often call personal evangelism is really an attempt at impersonal evangelism, i.e., a formulaic way of reaching people without really knowing them. Still another is the pushy intrusion of evangelical jargon into meetings and speeches, which triggers the fear in many people that one is proselytizing.

One thing that is necessarily involved in effective evangelism is flexibility. Each sociocultural context in which we minister is somewhat unique, and every person we meet is, in some ways, unique. So, effective evangelism is usually somewhat tailored to fit the person and the context. Furthermore, we evangelical Christians are not all alike in personality and giftedness, so we are called to engage in outreach in ways that are natural to us. So, granting these two reasons for flexibility in outreach, my top ten guidelines for reaching Democrats (and Republicans) are as follows:

1. Spending time with people, in their natural setting, while getting appropriately involved in their lives, and identifying with their good causes, would be pre-requisites to Christian evangelism in Democrat pop-ulations. People need to know that we know them (or want to know them), and that we understand them (or want to understand them), and that when they are right, or struggling, we are on their side. In every missionary setting, identifying with "the natives" is prerequisite to reaching them. When you join the local Democratic Party, don't expect to start at the top. You will pay your dues, stuff envelopes, and knock on doors like every other volunteer and in the company of other volunteers. Consider joining with several other people from your church (but only if you can avoid becoming a "Christian clique" within the local party organization). You could inter-cede for each other and for people you experienced a heart for; you could learn from each other's experi-ences, reflect with each other theologically, and wel-come seekers into your fellowship.

2. Spending time with people, listening to them, and identifying with their big concerns build bridges to pre-Christian people and, in time, to their families and to all the other people in their kinship and friendship networks. As Donald McGavran, father of the Church Growth movement taught us, people do not usually respond affirmatively to the Christian possibility if it is offered by a stranger. Social net-

works provide the bridges of God, and if the bridges to lost people who need to be found are not already in place, we need to build them—by making new friends.

3. We are called to love people (in the sense of willing the best for them) whether or not they (yet) affirm our faith. Most people are more loved than argued into the new life. We are called to model, in the political parties, the kind of compassionate diplomacy that treats everyone as a brother or sister with one common God, remembering that when we serve even the least of these we are meeting Christ himself, and that many people in both parties might need to see what loving one's enemies looks like.

4. In such relationships, while joined with others in common cause, we can experience the sacramental power of the ministry of conversation. From the cumulative effect of many conversations over time, conversations in which we are often listening about 80 percent of the time, many people will come to faith. This possibility increases if we can get them involved in conversation with several Christians. The market for one-way evangelical presentations (in which we preach at people for two minutes) has declined precipitously; the market for honest two-way conversations has never been greater. Let me add that it is usually possible to include God in the conversation. People are usually quite open to us praying with them. In one variation from simply praying with someone while we are with them, many Christians now contract to pray for someone. The Christian agrees to lift up the seeker's concern (say) each evening, while the seeker agrees to report any experiences in which God may be answering the prayer.

5. It is important to invite people to come to church with us. If we do, they will often find meaning or power in the music, the liturgy, the sermon, the art,

and/or the people who help them along the process. It may be even more important, for many people, to invite them into our Sunday school classes and small groups, or into our homes, where they can experience the ministry of hospitality—which is Christianity's most powerful way of communicating the gospel nonverbally.

6. Fairly early in our relationship with pre-Christian people, we need to be honest enough to tell them that *one* reason (but not the only reason) why we are now involved with Democrats is to share what has been entrusted to us for their sake—the gospel that, by God's grace through faith, would make them better Democrats, better people, kingdom people. Indeed, the life of faith-in-community will rescue them from the compassion fatigue that almost every person who commits to causes, but without an invisible means of support, experiences before their cause can prevail; people of faith can tap into the spiritual power that sustains them long enough to prevail.

7. Get involved long enough with the Democratic Party and you will meet some evangelical Christian Democrats who have served the party a long time while feeling abandoned, misunderstood, and sometimes lied about or even loathed by their fellow evangelical Christians who entered an (unnecessary) monogamous relationship with the other party. They will be encouraged by your presence and your companionship in common causes; in some cases, your presence will ratify their faith that may have wavered. You will also meet some liberal Christians who will, at first, be astonished that you are involved with the Democrats; in God's good time, they may be strangely attracted to a Christianity that is more deeply rooted in classical Christianity than they are used to, a faith deeply convinced that what Christi-

anity offers the human race is far more important than what any political party or government can offer.

8. If we get involved long enough, we will meet some Democrats who are ideologically committed to some cause, so committed that their cause functions as an idol—which they rely on to validate their lives and define their identity. How we perceive them is very important—for them. It is crucial for us to remember, especially when they are on a zealous streak, that if they have made their cause their ultimate reason for living, the cause will not meet the deepest needs of their souls. When they experience this fact, they may be receptive to Something Else. When we help such people (who are not allergic to strong commitment) to become Christ-followers, they often become the kind of radically committed Christians that our churches need more of.

9. With Democrats (as with Republicans) we can show them ways in which the Christian revelation is consistent with, validates, and deepens some of their beliefs and concerns. Indeed, as I have demonstrated above, it is possible to show that some Democratic causes are consistent with the understanding of the Will of God revealed in the prophets, and supremely in Jesus' teaching about the purposes of the kingdom of God that God wants fulfilled here on earth as they are in heaven. If they have experienced Stephen Neill's third conversion, show them that they may be nearer to the kingdom than they may have assumed.

10. Get involved long enough and you will befriend a pre-Christian political candidate or officeholder. Such persons, too, will often respond to our identification with some of their causes and as we show them the biblical roots for their causes. We may even get involved with an officeholder or aspirant who is already a Christian. When we help people learn to

integrate their faith with their life and worldview and coach them in better ways to articulate their faith, they can be greatly used in public affairs, and some will become bridges for reaching other people.

NOTES

1. Historically, the old rich and the new rich have had the most influence in the Republican Party, through contacts and contributions. They often send their kids to private schools, while cutting support for the public's schools. They are the greatest beneficiaries of Mr. Bush's "tax relief." Some of both groups are corporate barons or jet-setters who, they say, do not need to live by the same moral code as ordinary people. If they go to church, they make sure that their captive chaplain will be too nice to challenge their idols.

2. See George G. Hunter III, *Church for the Unchurched* (Nashville: Abingdon Press, 1995), chapter 2, "What People Can Become."

POSTSCRIPT: IF YOU ARE STILL RELUCTANT

E vangelical Christianity promises much more for the peoples of the United States than it has delivered in recent history. Though our churches have multiplied and our attendance has increased, we are not driven by the same redemptive vision that abolished slavery in the nineteenth century and undertook, in the early twentieth century, the evangelization of the world in this generation. You may or may not be convinced to join the Democrats, but I hope you are convinced that strategic evangelicals must not remain in the pocket of one party. For too long, the Republican Party has been able to take the support of evangelical Christians for granted; in return, they campaigned for election on some evangelical themes, but they have advanced little of the evangelical agenda in legislation.[1] In any case, we are called to befriend and love people within both parties, and to advocate what we understand to be God's will in both parties.

I should mention two tactical caveats.

First, I am not recommending that we politicize local churches; there is too much of that already. Specifically, a local church's pulpit is not the appropriate forum for a Christian leader's political advocacy (and a church's membership roll should not be available for any political party's use). The wider community provides many settings (such as party meetings, guest newspaper columns, door-to-door canvassing, and conversations in many settings) for Christian political advocacy. In any case, the most effective approach to political influence is conversation, not pontification.

Perhaps every Christian with a political conscience should be an active member of one of the political parties and a member of an organization or movement with a single cause that we believe in (such as, say, the NAACP or the Sierra Club or . . . the NRA, which could use more gun control advocates in its membership).

Nor, second, am I recommending that local churches (or denominations) risk becoming primary centers for political or social causes; there is too much of that already. The church's "main business" (to worship God, minister to people, reach pre-Christian people, root and build them in faith, and send them into the world as salt and light) is enormously more important than the agenda of any political party or social cause. Besides, when churches trade their main business for any other agenda, they are seldom effective. The most proven model for involving Christians in the world comes to us from the past—from such movements as abolitionist societies and mission societies. Such movements require such an advanced understanding of their cause, and such large numbers of people with an advanced commitment to that cause, that no church can do many causes justice, much less all of them. It is far more effective to root people in the gospel that grounds Christians in their primary identity, and to sensitize Christians to the range and depth of the kingdom's ethical vision, while expecting them to sign up for the party and cause for which they are most wired, informed, interested, and passionate.

I expect that some evangelical leaders will find my case plausible, but will struggle with the (now) obvious fact that more Republicans seem to profess faith than Democrats. How do we reflect upon that fact? How do we discern what to do? In addition to my obvious rejoinder—that Christians are specifically called to befriend, identify with, and reach people and groups who are not yet Christians, an oft-neglected parable from Jesus (in Matthew 21) provides a powerful perspective. A man who had two sons asked them to work in his vineyard. One son said he would not, but then he did it; the other son said he would, but he did not do it. Jesus then made his point through a memorable rhetorical question: "Which of the two did the will of his father?" Sometimes the Republicans are like the second son, and sometimes the Democrats are like the first son. In any case, the God we know in Jesus expects us to do his will on earth. Indeed, in the Sermon on the Mount, he notified us that "Not everyone who says to me 'Lord, Lord' shall enter the Kingdom of God, but he who does the will of my Father." Advancing his will in both parties is one reasonable way for us to be faithful.

Some evangelical Christian leaders remark that they see wisdom in much of what I have written, but they cringe at the thought of being associated with the Democratic Party's "lunatic fringe." While I understand the all-too-human reluctance to associate and fraternize with people who may not be like "good churchpeople" (as I explained much earlier), one version or another of this reluctance has limited the effectiveness of Christianity's mission much of the time, and in many places, since the second-century A.D. Christ calls us to practice a transcendent revolutionary love that dares to believe that any population, any person, matters to God and is reachable and redeemable.

In any case, Democrats have no monopoly on lunatic fringe people. The Klan and many other white supremacist groups, and many right-wing militia groups, and right-wing domestic terrorist groups (remember Oklahoma City?), and other anti-intellectual "flat earth" groups campaigned for Republicans (and/or against Democrats) in the 2004 election. I am told that such groups are more active in many state Republican Party organizations than ever before. So the only way to avoid fringe people is not to get involved with either party—which is not a valid option for people who Christ mandates to be involved in (but not of) the real (and fallen) world as salt and light. In any case, our grandparents used to say, "Politics makes strange bedfellows." That is often true, and the experience moves us out of our comfort zones and that makes political involvement even more interesting. If it is any consolation, in my involvements with some Democrats, I have sometimes noticed their discomfort when they discover that a professor of evangelism is in their company.

Evangelical Christianity's disengagement from Democrats a quarter century ago was the most strategically naïve step we could have taken. So permit me to extend an invitation to evangelical brothers and sisters. Like Mary of old, ponder these matters in your heart, collaborate with the people that help you make important decisions, and then get on board by doing three things: (1) Join, and become involved in, the party in which you could contribute the most; (2) Practice, model, and commend the civil, even compassionate, politics that needs to replace the rabid partisan beast that is now at loose in the land; (3) Do what you can to make becoming a Christ-follower a live option for the people you get involved with, and leave the rest to God. If you are hesitating, recall that Dante's hell reserves the hottest place for people who, in a time of crisis, remained neutral.

In time, you will experience a marvelous discovery—that following Christ in the world is the greatest adventure available in this life. Christians do not usually experience the meaning, richness, and power of that adventure, however, when they confine their activity to church and home. "God so loved the world," so we most experience the adventure in the world. The Christians who move out of their comfort zone, who care enough and dare enough to follow Jesus Christ in the world, experience him still multiplying loaves and fishes, and in time they experience the Bible's most extravagant promise: "No eye has seen, no ear has heard, no mind had conceived what God has prepared for those who love him" (1 Cor. 2:9-10 NIV).

NOTE

1. I am told that this is the reason that, in the 1990s, Jerry Falwell was much less involved with the Republican Party than he had been in the 1980s. More recently, in the 2004 campaign, President Bush aligned with the forces that advocate a constitutional amendment to protect marriage, but since the election, he appears to have lost interest.